BUILD A BETTER SPOUSE TRAP

BUILD A BETTER SPOUSE TRAP

A Street-Smart Dating Strategy for Men Who Have Lost a Love

Theodore S. Wentworth
with Lexi Welanetz, Psy.D.

M. Evans and Company, Inc.
New York

M. Evans and Company, Inc.
216 East 49th Street
New York, New York 10017

Library of Congress Cataloging-in-Publication Data

INSERT HERE

Book design and typesetting by Evan H. Johnston

To Diana and Sharon,
my two great loves, teachers, and cherished wives,
without whom this book would not have been possible.

CONTENTS

IV Into the Future

AUTHOR'S NOTE

I'm often asked about this book's provocative title. I generally refer to several lines in the classic Frank Sinatra song, "The Tender Trap":

Some starry night, when her kisses make you tingle
She'll hold you tight, and you'll hate yourself for being single
. . .
It's too late now, there's no gettin' out
You fell in love, and love is the tender trap

Those words say it all. When that exciting new person sweeps into your life and you feel love—real love—it's a wonderful, powerful, magnetic energy. It perks up your life and causes you to feel different and better about everything. Do you want it to stop? Do you want to return to the way you felt before? Do you want to be free from that feeling? No! And there you have it—the tender "trap."

Most men, especially those who've experienced a painful loss of love, hope they'll fall into that tender trap again someday. This book is about how to make it happen, how to turn hope into reality. It's about developing an intelligent strategy—a deliberate, purposeful plan—for finding that special new partner and best friend. It's all about how you, or anyone, can "build a better spouse trap."

Build a Better Spouse Trap can be, and I trust will be, a wise companion. I know about the hurt you're experiencing, and I'm offering you a proven strategy that can help you handle that hurt and restore joy to your life.

—TED WENTWORTH

FOREWORD

Straight talk will never go out of style, and this remarkable book offers straight talk at its best. *Build a Better Spouse Trap* is written specifically for men, yet because of the insight it provides, women will also find it extremely interesting and provocative.

If you are—or are close to—a man who has lost a love, the title and subtitle have already told you this book is exactly what you want. It will help you deal not only with the immediate pain of loss from death or divorce, but also with the longer-term grief that inevitably follows. Grief that carries anger, guilt, and depression—feelings you must understand if you are to handle them successfully. This book is a terrific guide to sorting out and resolving those difficult emotions.

Getting fully back into life after this kind of devastating personal loss includes finding another mate. In these pages, you'll discover a practical strategy for meeting that all-important new person. In fact, even if you haven't lost a love, you'll find that this book is a brilliant, state-of-the-art guide to adult dating. So if you're simply seeking a high-quality partnership, *Build a Better Spouse Trap* is also for you.

My friend Ted Wentworth knows what he's talking about. He is a nationally acclaimed trial lawyer who specializes in medical, human rights, sexual harassment, and employment issues, which means that his everyday, professional associations keep him in contact with the practical side of male-female relationships and interpersonal issues. He knows his stuff—both the theory and the practice. But in a book like this, theories take someone just so far. Life experience and street savvy are what make the critical difference. When you read these pages, you'll know the author has an ample supply of both.

In *Build a Better Spouse Trap*, you'll hear Ted Wentworth as a straight-talking professional, and you'll also come to know him personally, as a man with deep feelings. You'll experience his true heart—which is also the heart of this book—in his caring and kindness, in his feelings for and about women, in his attention to both the sweeping broadstrokes and fine brushwork of developing and nurturing an intimate personal relationship. You'll recognize Ted as a smart, practical guy who deeply cares about people and who, in particular, genuinely loves, respects, and appreciates women.

With deep feeling, Ted describes his struggle to regain his balance after his wife of twenty-two years died of cancer. His love and caring are evident when he describes how he went searching for—and finally found—his new "best friend and wife," *the* woman he wanted so profoundly to bring into his life. His canny intelligence is apparent in the strategy he developed on his way to finding her. (He methodically checked out 130 other candidates first.) It's a strategy he describes in detail, so you can reap the benefits of everything he learned.

Here then, from a man whose mind and heart abound with both practicality and wisdom, are the real-life facts you'll wish your father had given you when you were starting to date. They are also the very things you may wish you'd been able to—or still can—tell your son or nephew or grandson when he starts to date and move into adult relationships. In fact, the information in this book is timeless, and you wouldn't be off-base to give a copy to every person you know.

Ted Wentworth knew how to look for the woman his heart was yearning for . . . and he found her. We're lucky he decided to pass his secrets along to the rest of us.

—JACK CANFIELD, *co-author,*
Chicken Soup for the Soul *series*

ACKNOWLEDGMENTS

Few things are as important in the life of a man as the women who are in it with him. For me, at the top of my list are my extraordinary wife Diana, my daughters Kathryn and Christina, and Diana's daughter Lexi Welanetz, who wrote this book with me.

Diana constantly inspires me with her talent and ability as a writer, and I admired her many published books for years before I ever thought of writing my own. In supporting me during this project, she was what she has been all along since the day we met: remarkable, gorgeous, graceful, extraordinary, and beyond comparison.

Christy and Kathy—now adults who are as lovely and bright as they were growing up—have taught me so much about love, about what women want out of life, and about how to prioritize what's important.

Lexi is a beautiful woman whose training and experience as a psychologist specializing in couples counseling perfectly equipped her to fill a major role in supervising the manuscript. I brought a lifetime of personal and professional experience with people—people struggling with life's challenges—to the heart of it. But when I needed help in *her* field, when I needed to look more deeply into psychological issues or to explore modern therapeutic concepts more thoroughly, I sought her invaluable counsel. She was my authority in those areas—if not always sitting with me at my writing table, then no more than a phone call away. She reviewed the manuscript at every stage, conferring with me regularly and making me the beneficiary of her expertise. I am happy to take overall responsibility for what appears here, but without her this would not have been the book it is, a book of which she and I are extremely proud.

The parents of my sons-in-law, Court Purdy, Jeff Coyne, and David Bursin, have also inspired me by being models of successful family relationships.

I've learned that a book is born of more than just the creativity and devotion of its author, for that author stands on the shoulders of many teachers, both personal and professional. My most profound personal teachers have been the women I noted above, as well as yet another . . . my late wife Sharon, who was the sweetest part of my life for twenty-two years and who left me to Diana reasonably housebroken.

Professionally, the advice, counsel, and suggestions from my primary editor, Hadley Fitzgerald, MFT, were the magic that helped me deliver what I wanted to say in the right way. Her great heart, kindness, patience, outstanding command of language, and therapeutic savvy added greatly to my bragging rights as a first-time author.

Just when I thought the manuscript was complete, I consulted freelance editor John Niendorff, whose excellent suggestions made the work even easier to read.

Margie M. Mirell, MFT, and Wiley B. Johnson, Ph.D., graciously reviewed and improved the manuscript by offering suggestions and helping me think through some important distinctions related to social challenges faced by men. I am grateful for their wisdom.

Nancy Fehrmann was exceptionally kind in offering her time and professional knowledge, making available to me her enormous fund of information about sexually transmitted diseases.

Judy Foley of Connaissance generously provided valuable insight on the subject of Internet dating and executive dating services.

Many other people from various walks of life were kind enough to read the manuscript at different stages of its development, and over two dozen made suggestions, most of which are included in the completed work. Thanks to Kathy Juline, to P.G., and to my two final readers, Bobbie Probstein and Ann Hartley, who were brilliant in spotting minute details the rest had overlooked.

My two law partners—William M. Delli Paoli, J.D., and Court B. Purdy, J.D.—offered me their constant encouragement, as did my fellow lawyer-author Kevin Gallagher, J.D., for which I was and am most thankful.

And I gratefully acknowledge Peter Wernicke, J.D., family lawyer to the people, for permitting me to publish his premarital agreement.

Thanks to Linda Algazi, Ph.D., for helping me develop the valuable information on men, women, and money. And to Melanie Rigney of *Writer's Digest*, my thanks for that one perfect word that transformed an easily misunderstood paragraph into perfection.

I especially appreciate my caring and supportive agent, Carole Bidnick, for her comprehensive knowledge of the publishing world, and also George deKay, Harry McCullough, Rik Schell, and Amy Koch of the staff at M. Evans and Company, Publishers, who tactfully and effectively contributed their expertise to this project. And a big thank you to the wonderful sales force at National Book Network—you're the best!

Advance applause to Jill Siegel, who, along with the promotion team at M. Evans, will carry this work to its highest potential.

Finally, I gratefully acknowledge several groups of people. First, the men and women who have been close to me in business during my professional career; they expanded my understanding about the simplicity of integrity. Second, all who served me as secretaries and office assistants during my forty years of law practice—especially the women, who added their invaluable insights to my understanding of the demands placed on professional women. Sharon Glommen, Paula Ward, and Mary LaRue influenced me greatly in this regard. And third, my thousands of clients during those same four decades, who taught me so much about love and the wondrous complexity of human nature.

Life is either a daring adventure or nothing.
—Helen Keller

INTRODUCTION

HOME ALONE

Like so many men, when I first married I was very self-focused. I was "me," and my wife Sharon was one of many "objects" I had acquired to fulfill me. As our relationship developed into a deep and genuine connection over the years, I realized that I was part of a "we"—we were partners in each other's lives. I also grew to realize that developing good relationships is a *skill*, and as I looked around me, I noticed that some people had more skill than others.

Since I greatly respect the power of education, I decided to immerse myself in a study of relationships, especially my relationship with Sharon. In learning ways to fulfill *her*, and eventually our children, I learned that there is a bigger payoff in *giving* love than getting it. When I gave love without caring whether or not I got it back, it just came back by itself—often in wonderful, unpredictable ways. This discovery brought new gifts to my soul, and my life became richer. Sharon grew too, and proceeded to improve her own relationship skills. Our last fifteen years together were the sweetest, coziest, most wonderful experience—the stuff dreams are made of.

Then she died, and I didn't.

It took longer than I expected to get to the other side of the oppressive grief and the multilayered adjustments that followed Sharon's death from breast cancer. Then, two and a half years after she died, I married my talented and beautiful wife Diana, who had lost her first husband to cancer. I learned my lessons well over the two years that I dated some wonderful women and eventually qualified to be, and to have, a new best friend, lover, and spouse. I found a deep connection again. It doesn't get any sweeter than this.

I know there are a lot of men whose experiences more or less parallel my own in terms of losing a love. I also know that men would benefit from knowing what I learned about dealing with grief, about enhancing personal relationships, and, finally, about searching for and finding another life-companion, another "Mrs. Right-For-Me" (as opposed to just another "Ms. Right-Now"). Plenty of qualified women are out there. Many of them feel quite alone and are praying for someone who is right for them. You can be an answer to those prayers by learning how to be the right one. When you do, you'll see a miracle unfold.

If, like me, you've suffered the loss of your mate and best friend through death—or divorce—you've experienced the demise of your old identity. You are now pure potential. You wonder, "Who am I now?" And then you think, "I'm not the kid who got married years ago. I'm not always going to be the man who just lost his mate. I need to know about grief, I need to know more about myself, and I'd like another chance to be a good partner."

You may still love the story you lived, but the final chapter has been written. You are now poised to open a whole new *book*. To make that possible, you will need to see farther than you can at this time. You'll need to ask yourself certain new questions.

What's going on in your life now? What are the parts you want to change? What parts *don't* you want to change? What can you do to rediscover yourself? What's happened in the mating dance during the years you've been out of circulation? How do you let go and go beyond what you had? How do you deal with the fear of making those kinds of changes? Other, more specific questions deserve your attention also. How can you avoid being fooled by a woman's superficial allure? When do you need a "coach," and how do you find one? You know love and sex are deal breakers, but how does money (or the lack of it) fit in?

Let me offer you insight, analysis, and a plan.

Coping with Loss

This section's two chapters look at *grief*—the pain you feel when you've lost a love. This pain follows any wrenching separation, especially death or divorce. Here are several simple, powerful ways to move yourself more quickly through the five stages of grief, so you can get on with your life.

Healing your anguish settles the past and opens your future—perhaps not with optimism or even great expectations at first, but your future *does* become important to you again.

Section I contains essential insights about recovering from grief and moving on. Regardless of which ones you choose, you'll get a deep look at who you are, and at what you want to do now.

So hang in there. Trust me—the pain will go away and you will create a new life.

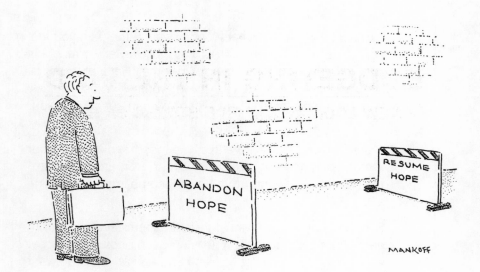

Where you used to be, there is a hole in the world, which I find myself constantly walking around in the daytime, and falling in at night. I miss you like hell.
—Edna St. Vincent Millay

1

BOOGEYING IN THE VOID
A NEW LOOK AT THE FIVE STAGES OF GRIEF

The loss of your mate through death or divorce is profound. If you have a great capacity for intimacy and for loving others, you feel as if something inside of *you* has been torn away, too. Through death or divorce, you have lost your lover and possibly your best friend and the mother of your beautiful children. The cut is deep and your pain torments you as an elusive, indelible emptiness. Your defense mechanisms hide the extent of your emotional damage. That damage will intensely color your outlook in the years ahead. But if you *hurt* deeply because you *feel* deeply, that's an asset for you in the long run.

Losing your wife through death is different than losing her through divorce, because death is a final goodbye and divorce is not. The grief in both death and divorce may *feel* the same, but death is usually surrounded by ritual, social understanding, and collective approval of your uncertain steps toward recovery. With her no longer physically present, death demands that you move on. Divorce, however, brings neither that sense of acceptance nor that kind of clarity in the community.

With divorce, your relationship has died, but not your spouse. Your former wife continues to be a living reminder of what was or could have been. The grief from divorce is contaminated by what's left unresolved in the ongoing relationship. Numerous practical changes must still be discussed and then implemented in your life—financial arrangements, splitting of residence, custody of children, visitation agreements, and so on—almost as if nothing tragic had happened. And despite our high divorce rate, society still has not developed any rituals to provide for closure and a sense of moving on afterward. So you're left with the feeling that the marriage has been legally terminated but has not truly ended.

I won't dwell on the various complications that make a divorce different from a death, because this book is focused on how to move on regardless of the conditions of your loss. However, be aware that most of us would have differing responses when told that the man weeping here in this corner has just lost his wife to cancer and the man weeping over there in that corner has just gotten his final divorce papers. Both men are deeply wounded, yet we as a society have different expectations of them. If you are among the divorced men reading this book, know that everything I say applies to you. Just recognize that emotionally, your divorce is similar to a death, because your marriage is over—regardless of how it happened.

In my experience, men are more accepting of physical injuries than emotional ones. We understand them. Physical injuries are something we can see and then take practical, logical steps to heal. Emotional wounds are different. They can't be seen and can't be healed with the same methods. But emotional wounds cause just as much agony as physical ones. Further, while the pain of a physical injury is felt only at the site of the injury, an emotional wound is felt throughout our entire being—in the head, the heart, and the gut. The deeper the emotional wound, the greater the agony. And the effects of the damage caused by this wound stream into your life and into the lives of those close to you.

In some ways the two kinds of injuries are the same. They both heal from the inside out. Emotional healing begins deep inside, in your silence, below the level of your awareness. You can heal your troubled feelings layer by layer, by examining and dealing with them as they come to the surface during your daily activities.

After Sharon died, I would wake up in the morning and stare in disbelief at the four walls. No one was there beside me. Suddenly my lady and best friend was gone. I felt like the most delicate parts of my heart had gone with her. I still had a huge love inside me, and for the first time in twenty-two years had no one to give it to.

Not only was I lonely, but I also felt *guilty*. Sharon died over a four-year period, a millimeter at a time. She knew I was going to live. She knew I was going to have a new life and she wasn't. She knew she would not see our daughters marry, nor would she see our grandchildren—and I would. I saw all of that in her eyes during the many quiet moments between us. After she died, more guilt stared me down. Guilt for feeling relieved because I got to stay when she couldn't. Big guilt over not being able to give her the gift of life she wanted so badly. Guilt over how gracious she was about all of it. Guilt in feeling relieved that the agony of our day-to-day struggle was over—at least I thought it was. And guilt because . . . well, the guilt was just endless and it didn't need a reason.

I missed her terribly—but gradually I realized that I didn't want to go through life with a cold empty space on the bench next to me. Sharon told me several times during her long illness that she wanted me to be happy and to go on. Even with my memories of her saying that, the possibility of "dating" again, especially in midlife and after so many years of marriage, was very difficult to face. "Why go on?" is a question I often asked myself. Besides, my generation regards dating as something that kids do. But succumbing to self-pity was not like me. I'd always picked myself up, dusted myself off, and gone on with my life.

Your response to your loss will be unique. One man will want to sit back for a time, while another will seek companionship early on.

How long will your emotional pain last? Some suggest that you'll need a year to recover for every five you were together. Regardless, the first year will be, by far, the worst. Every significant day or holiday offers an emotional challenge—and not necessarily in any form you can predict. Learn to be kind to yourself on those occasions.

I expected to have a rough time on the first Valentine's Day without Sharon, because it had been one of our favorite holidays. I braced myself emotionally, and to my surprise, it went fine. So I figured I was all done with the grief. But on Mother's Day, three months later, and eleven months after Sharon's passing, I was hosting a family luncheon at a local restaurant when suddenly I was overwhelmed with a sinking feeling. Within minutes, I was physically ill, emotionally disconnected from the party, and unable to continue. I held myself together the best I could and excused myself immediately following dessert. I went directly home to bed, where I curled up in the fetal position and slept for four hours. I was baffled. It was just a luncheon, and I had already been dating for six months. Where did these feelings come from? I felt weak and exhausted, like I had been hit with the flu. Bed, a pillow over my head, tears, and a four-hour nap, followed by a discussion with my friends about what had happened, were all a great help.

In the years since Sharon's death I've spoken with many friends who've lost loved ones. All of them could tell more than one story about being hit by what they called "the bolt out of the blue." My new wife, Diana, experienced such feelings over the loss of her husband and referred to them as "getting hit by a pie in the face." So it's normal for such occurrences to hit you on unpredictable dates and occasions. Just be patient—the bad feelings pass.

So be prepared. You will find that the grief you thought you'd left behind still lurks in the shadows. You'll find that your loss has had a much greater effect on you than you realize. Your grief carries with it a *top-heavy* load of guilt, anger, despair, and lethargy that, if ignored, robs you of your vitality. You feel worn-down, irritable, and depressed as you attempt to balance your grief and hide it—from yourself and from your world.

Does this sound familiar? Are you doing it even now? If you are, then you're still denying—blocking or walling off—your feelings of loss. If you're not visibly crying, you're crying inside. You are stunned, numb, and preoccupied. *You are still not feeling.* You've lost much of your sensitivity and your capacity to interact with your surroundings.

Death-and-dying expert Elisabeth Kübler-Ross, M.D., has written beautifully, for both the layperson and the professional, about the five stages of grief. Familiar to many, they are: *denial, anger, bargaining, depression,* and *acceptance.* They tend to show up pretty much in that order, but they might piggyback one another or move back and forth. In other words, you can feel fully immersed in both depression and denial or suddenly flip from depression back into denial. Let's examine how understanding and working through these five stages can eventually help open a place in your life for a new mate.

DENIAL

Think of denial as a temporary seal over an overwhelming emotional wound. Now picture that seal with a slow leak that allows the pain to seep from the wound a little at a time. You can see how denial is a valuable and protective defense mechanism to help you deal with great pain in quantities you can handle. Yet lingering in denial will unnecessarily prolong the effects of unresolved grief and damage your future.

It's important for you to be able to recognize when you're in denial. Denial always comes up on your blind side. For instance, impending divorce brews like heavy weather. Probably both partners are unhappy—perhaps for years—but when one of them finally says the "D word," everything that's been lurking in the background becomes real, and the effect is emotionally devastating. Both are jolted and dazed and withdraw into denial—no longer experiencing their deeper feelings while they figure out where to put the blame, who will live where, and what to tell the children.

Whether it's death or divorce, whether it comes suddenly or slowly, the actual event arrives by surprise. Sharon's death was anticipated for at least two of the four years she was ill, but when it finally happened, I watched my whole family go into shock. And then immediately into denial.

Our reaction was obvious the day of the funeral. Looking back now, I can see that our denial peaked at the gathering immediately following her service. About 200 friends and associates had gathered at our home. Everyone seemed happy. My two girls, Christina and Kathryn, appeared to be beaming with joy. They and their friends put streamers all over the family car, and we all felt it was the best party we'd ever had—a celebration of Sharon's life. We tied helium balloons around the perimeter of our patio so everyone could release a balloon before leaving. We followed each balloon with our hearts as it climbed alone into the sky and disappeared into the distance, carried by a soft breeze from the Pacific just three miles away. It was a beautiful, sunny June afternoon. It was very sweet . . . and we were *all* in denial.

Widowed or divorced, early on you may have a little voice in your head saying, "Oh, this isn't so bad. It's actually *good* to have some time to myself again. I can go to bed whenever I like, I don't have to eat on time, and I can eat anything I want. I don't have to fix anything or clean up afterward. I can see all the violent flicks I want and even watch the late show. I have control of the remote, and she has no say whether I sleep in late or floss my teeth. I never want to live with anyone again—it's too complex. I'm enjoying my sovereignty and my solitude!"

Listen to that voice—it's the sound of denial.

It is a voice that can't be trusted, because it is part of a walling-off process that adds dangerous potential to your new life. Stuffing your feelings down so deeply that you can't feel them is the equivalent of barricading them with bricks and mortar. This may later cause uncharacteristic behavior that seems to erupt out of nowhere: raging at a waiter because the coffee isn't hot enough or missing a crucial business meeting because you simply "forgot." Or perhaps withdrawal from family, friends, and your favorite activities, accompanied by a closer but unhealthy relationship with your preferred alcoholic beverage.

Stuffing or walling off may appear to be the "strong" thing to do—keep a stiff upper lip, be brave, and all that—but it's not going to get you where you want to go. Stuffed feelings, rather than improving your life, snowball into even greater pain and embarrassing emotional outbursts. And that's why this isn't a book about being strong. It's a book about healing—recovering from a tremendous emotional blow. Most of us who think of ourselves as *men* find it very disconcerting to be walking down the street and suddenly feel tears running down our cheeks. Though such an experience is a healthy release, our natural reaction is to decide that we won't get blindsided by such emotional "weakness" again. Then we kick our feelings deeper into the shutdown mode, both publicly and in private. Shutting down means we wall off our feelings, emotionally disconnecting from ourselves, from our environment, and especially from those close to us. We think we're doing well when actually we've simply adjusted our mask to fit better by withdrawing and insulating ourselves even more.

Our bodies and souls are wonderfully resilient; with a little encouragement they will go a long way toward healing themselves. However,

I want to plant a seed in your mind, here. Now, or sometime soon, take a moment to look at chapter 11 (page 135) of this book. That chapter, "The Therapist as a Resource: For Me or for Us," is where I let you in on all that I learned about the value of being coached by a professional. We men often dismiss any thought of seeing a "shrink" or a therapist or "head coach" or counselor—my friends sure did until they discovered just how much they *didn't* know about how valuable a professional could be.

MENTAL EXERCISES FOR GRIEF RELIEF

If you can't quite decide whether or not you want to see a professional, here are three techniques to help you deal with unresolved grief. You'll probably find one or more of them helpful. They all involve *attention*. Your healing process will accelerate once you learn to place your attention on your pain. Your attention, focused on an aspect of your grief, can, by itself, heal you without any further effort on your part. So, you ask, how do you put your attention on your pain?

Notice how you can move your attention around. Try putting your attention on the end of your nose. Once you're aware of your nose, move your awareness (attention) to your right big toe. Now to your left shoulder blade. Finish by focusing it on the top of your head. Notice how easily your attention moves around? Now go to the techniques that follow.

Technique #1: Focus your attention on the source of your grief. Gather together photographs and any other memorabilia that might trigger strong feelings. Take them, along with a box of Kleenex, into a secluded area of your house—or drive to a private spot and park. Have the box of Kleenex at hand, place the nostalgic items on your lap, and start a conversation with them. Talk to them—and listen to what they want to say to you. Through this process your attention gains access to your feelings of anguish, anger, despair, sadness, and loneliness.

For me, talking to the person in the photo, out loud or by just thinking the words, immediately accessed strong, previously blocked feelings. I allowed myself at least one ten-minute grieving retreat daily, until I honestly felt I had healed some pretty heavy emotional stuff. Later I reduced these "sessions" to twice a week, then once a week, and finally once a month. I quit the exercise when I felt I was pretty steady, but I returned to it whenever I was feeling emotional again. If nothing was there to fix, I wouldn't experience much of a release, but occasionally I was surprised. This is a good technique because it's safe and private, and if you use it, your emotional stability will improve immeasurably. There's such grace in allowing tears to help clear out your unresolved grief. If you can't access that part of yourself—if no tears appear, if relief seems impossible—strong denial may be preventing your experiencing an emotional release. A therapist will know how to help you heal your heart.

Technique #2: This is a clever tool that is most powerful when you don't try to make sense of it. It's a well-known Gestalt psychology method that very gently moves your attention onto your feelings and the effect they have on you.

Sit down, close your eyes, and get comfortable. Cup both hands together in front of you just above your lap, as though you are holding a tennis ball. Now, in your imagination, picture your grief cupped in your hands—picture it as an object or perhaps a little animal. How big is it? How does it feel? What is it made of? Is it fuzzy or smooth? What color is it? What is its temperature? How much does it weigh? Can you talk to it? What does it say? As you consider the object in this way, does it change—perhaps by getting smaller, lighter, maybe different in color? Usually, within a few minutes, it gets smaller, lighter, and easier to be with, and it will probably talk with you before it leaves.

I am aware that it is one thing for me to offer you a technique and quite another for you to feel comfortable using it. A "head coach" can assist you with it in the beginning. Such guided practice will encourage you to use the technique privately when you feel the need.

Technique #3: This one is easy. Write letters. Direct your attention to your discomfort by writing to your late or former partner—or to your feelings. Consider this a journal-writing technique that you can use to converse with others or any aspect of yourself. Speak to them in your writing and let them talk back: "Dear Joan, I want you to know how I'm feeling with you gone." Describe your anger, loneliness, disappointment, fear, resentment, and the like. Does she reply to you in your writing? Do certain aspects of yourself, such as your anger or fear or loneliness, respond?

When you've done this, finish with a paragraph about forgiveness. Write the letter in a single sitting; when you've covered everything you can think of, then *burn the letter* in a safe place. As you do, visualize all the pain and the "baggage" it represents being consumed by the flames. Every time you write such a letter your grief should gradually fade, becoming less and less, until you're finally clear of it. This writing contains your emotional junk—never mail it to anyone!

These and other such practices will help you gain more clarity about your feelings. Regardless of how well the techniques do or don't work, it is a good idea to get help from a therapist who will validate your experience and encourage you in your healing process. Consider time with your therapist as a *fourth* technique for putting your attention on your pain and the emotional shifts you're experiencing.

SUPPORT GROUPS

With a little effort, you'll find "survivor" support groups or opportunities for group counseling in your community. Local hospitals, religious centers, and the like should be able to direct you. Whether you find the groups great, or boring and useless, will be up to you. Many men find survivor groups invaluable. (Groups are also easier on your budget than one-on-one therapy.)

The opportunity to be with other men and women who, like you, have lost a loved one, and who are themselves coping with painful feelings, can be invaluable. Working with others in this way can lead to greater comfort, deeper understanding, released emotions, and a sense of shared humanity that is unavailable when you're working alone. If the thought of a support group, group counseling, or coach/therapist makes you want to run for your cave, I urge you to recognize that we men tend to isolate ourselves and think that asking for support is a sign of weakness. Therefore I suggest that you make up your own mind—check groups out for yourself.

Whether or not you realize what's happening, if you allow your unexamined emotions and stuffed feelings to smolder within you, they will distract your attention and play havoc with your memory and your ability to concentrate—and numb your heart. Your deepening and *unrecognized* preoccupation with your pain will distance you from all but your closest friends and family. People want to feel you're with them, but you will seem self-absorbed. You won't be good company again until you regain your ability to connect with others, with their interests and *their* environment. For those who don't feel comfortable with you—forgive them. They don't know how to reach out to you, and won't tell you so. They just back away. *You're* the last to know you've "disappeared." And that's very hard on everyone—including you.

Habitually walling off your feelings leads to a progressive loss of control of your emotions and your life, and this continues until you hit bottom and crash. That is a very distressing adventure, one that takes different forms for different people. But the good news is that having hit bottom, you can push off for a new start.

You don't need to suffer the crash—or the attendant loss of your ability to function—if you *examine* your grief instead of walling it off. A coach helps here by offering you perspective on your suffering. With perspective, you can see where you are and what needs to be done next.

A BRIEF EXPEDITION INTO THE MONKEY MIND

I was still hurting deeply six months after Sharon's death. The walls of denial were slowly coming down, allowing me to experience my grief a little at a time. However, my "monkey mind" was going nuts—and yours will probably do the same.

Let me introduce the monkey mind. I've learned to regard its behavior as a measure of my overall emotional health. This "mind" is an aspect of your internal dialogue. It's the "chatterbox," the "radio voice," "stinkin' thinkin'," the "critical voice," and so on. We all have this nutty voice in our *heads*—not our hearts. In routine daily life, the voice of the monkey mind makes comments of the worst kind, preoccupying us like a midnight mosquito in the bedroom.

Tune in to your mind-riot while you're walking down the street. You might observe such thoughts as: "Look at him—doesn't he think he's wonderful? If he just knew how stupid he looks with that haircut. That bimbo over there needs her mother to dress her. Look at that makeup. What's that dog doing over there—I'll bet the guy isn't going to clean it up—what an ugly jerk." The possibilities are endless. If anyone else could actually tune in and hear this mental monologue, you'd be embarrassed. Its observations are worthless, and its suggestions are so negative and demeaning that taking even a small percentage of them seriously would be impossible.

You can assess the impact of your monkey mind in this time of grief by observing the following: Do you go to work and just sit there? Have you lost your ability to recall telephone numbers and to focus on tasks before you? Does your mind-chatter say, "I'm doing all right, I'm not affected by what's happened, I'm still my old self"? Later, in moments of quiet, it will continue: "I'm fine—so what if the relationship evaporated [into death or divorce]. Nothing's really changed—this isn't such a big deal. Maybe it's a good time to go somewhere else and start over. The change will be good for the kids. [Or, worse: 'The kids can manage without me.'] I just want people to leave me alone. They can be so thoughtless. They just don't understand." And on and on and on. The monkey mind *loves* to masquerade and loves to play with your denial. Trust me—you can't trust it.

My friend John lost his wife to cancer after she had the disease for only eight months. His monkey mind chewed away at him: "I can't stand my old house. I can't stand my job. I've lived here all my life and everything I see reminds me of her. It's better that I move far away. Maybe I'll move to the country, where there's a well to drink from. I'm doing okay. If I wasn't, I'd know it."

I took John to dinner and tried to warn him about the voice, but he was convinced it was his "intuition." Within three months he'd sold everything he owned in Southern California and moved to a farmhouse—with a well—in Wisconsin. And he lost everything. Everything! That voice in his head was not his friend. And the move had a profoundly negative effect on his nearly grown children as well. At a time like that, the chatter of the monkey mind is easily mistaken for wisdom or intuition. Wisdom it's not. And genuine intuition is *not* a voice—it's a knowing in the heart.

When we're "on the bounce," we can easily convince ourselves that it's a good idea to quit our job, sell our house, leave all our furniture, and move to a new town—because we deserve a fresh start, right? You already know not to make decisions when your judgment is clouded. That's what happened to John. These actions and decisions don't feel impulsive, but they are. Even though we believe we're okay, the seal of denial is still covering our overloaded emotions *and* our good judgment.

Remember when you've eaten or drunk too much or engaged in some kind of mischief you later regretted? The voice that prompted you to do so was the monkey mind. Reflecting upon such an experience you might hear yourself saying, "Well, it seemed like a good idea at the time." The same thing is happening when you're reeling from grief. The seduction by your monkey mind "feels" so logical and trustworthy—but it most assuredly is not. And now is not the time to listen to it.

Wherever you go, there you are! There's no running away—no escape from you. *You* are your problem. Widowed or divorced, many a man like our friend John has been seduced by this insane monkey into making major changes while he was still in the grieving process. It's true that you might have strong inner reserves that are capable of ignoring the voice. But—after a string of weak moments—the voice's "advice" can seem like an idea whose time has come.

In creating a new life, you want to be proactive rather than reactive. Therefore, a good rule is: do nothing now. Make as few changes as possible until the first year is behind you. After that, you're better able to discriminate between the monkey mind's incessant, unrelenting, unreliable chatter and the quiet, more reliable *knowing* in your heart—what men sometimes refer to as a "gut feeling."

As your grief dissolves, your judgment will clear. You'll be more able to recognize your heart's desire. Until then, your grief not only colors your gut feelings, intuition, and insight, but also *stimulates* your untrustworthy internal dialogue.

So, regardless of the monkey mind's dictates, do not quit your job, move to another city, or forget that you are "on the bounce." If something big feels like a good idea now, and it truly is, then it will be an even better idea later, after your emotions have healed and your good judgment has returned. Furthermore, you don't want to make decisions based on your old ways or the old you. The inner healing work you'll be doing will position you for your new life, for the new you being born as you read this. Let the new you—free of grief—make the new choices.

ANGER

Anger arising from your grief is another threat to sound judgment, as it contributes more fuel to the monkey mind's madness. While anger may not surprise a man in the process of divorce, it might completely sneak up on a man who has recently been widowed. Grief-driven anger is damaging to your relationships with others. It separates you from family and business associates. They don't understand what's happening to you. They don't realize you are still grieving and that anger is one of the symptoms. They may back away from you and wall *themselves* off against your hurtful outbursts. Thus, anger effectively cuts the grieving victim from the pack, his life changes for the worse, and he doesn't know why.

At times, while discussing something with business associates or friends just after Sharon died, I could go from calmness to rage in a remarkably short period of time. I would fly into a torrent of self-righteousness. I was right and felt certain that everyone else was wrong. This was a new kind of behavior for me.

For example, a year after Sharon died I bought a new car. I'd handed over my check in full payment for it, but as I was taking delivery, the folks at the dealership tried to hide the fact that the car they were delivering had a damaged door. When I rejected the car, they refused to return my check and insisted that I accept the car. After all, they reasoned, they could fix the door in a day. I launched into such a rage over their unreasonableness that three police cars were summoned to quell the disturbance.

What poor judgment on my part! Afterwards, I realized that all I had to do was call the bank and stop payment on the check. What was the big deal? But there I was, discovering that unresolved (unexamined) grief was as dangerous as I'd been told. What a shock! Because of Sharon's four-year illness, I believed I had grieved *before* she died and that now I was through with grieving. Sound familiar? I was very, very wrong.

During the denial stage, we stuff—or push—our feelings below the level of awareness. Those pressurized feelings expand with time and make us work uncomfortably hard to contain them. Then, in a moment when our defenses are weakened or relaxed, those stuffed feelings can erupt as anger. Suddenly you have an ugly reaction to something quite benign. It leaps out at the most inopportune moment—like a frog onto the table. This embarrassing new behavior is a sign that you've pushed too much grief down below the level of your feelings instead of healing it by paying attention to it, examining it, feeling it.

If you don't examine and experience your grief, it floods in during vulnerable moments when you don't have enough energy or presence of mind to control it. The eruption of intense anger and other strong, surprising emotions or behavior three months to a year after your loss cry out for professional help. Getting help at a time like this isn't a sign of weakness. It is the brave, heroic, strong thing to do. (Please preview chapter 11.)

BARGAINING

The bargaining stage—the third ingredient in the grief process—comes next. It creates the illusion that you could have altered someone else's life or the outcome of an overwhelming event, if only you had behaved differently. In the bargaining stage of grief over losing a love, you may have heard yourself saying, "God, if you will only ____, I promise never to ____ again." "If you will spare her life [bring her back, save our marriage], then I will ____." This negotiating carries with it huge amounts of guilt that lead to self-criticism and the lament, "If I had just been a better husband, she wouldn't have died [or left]."

The self-examination that comes with this stage is instructive. If you are dealing with divorce, an analysis of what you might have done to prevent the divorce may be needed. It might improve your sensitivity and behavior as you move on to new relationships.

My advice at this stage is to be as straightforward and compassionate with yourself as possible. Recognize where you genuinely knew better and chose to ignore it. Then let the rest go. Forgive yourself for being human. If you're still uncomfortable, find a coach who can teach you how to be a self-correcting missile.

DEPRESSION

Bargaining temporarily holds the depression monster at bay. Once bargaining fails to change anything that's happened, you are left with your powerlessness and the awful reality of your current circumstances. That tips most of us over into depression—a temporary and perfectly appropriate reaction to your situation. Depression shows up as feelings of sadness, detachment, indecisiveness, lethargy, hopelessness, flatness, diminished interest in sex, inability to focus or concentrate, memory loss, change in appetite, low self-esteem, and altered sleeping patterns.

There are varying medical opinions on treating situational depression with medication. A substantial body of thought holds that prescription drugs, alcohol, or avoidant behavior delay your healing. You heal by examining the "emotional junk" generated by the tragedy. And you clear grungy feelings by addressing your grief head-on—by expressing and moving through the feelings, not by stuffing them further out of sight with the help of medication or alcohol.

Nevertheless, your doctor may offer antidepressants, even if other health-care professionals disagree. I support the use of antidepressants only as a temporary means of coping while you continue to address the issues with a therapist—and *only* if you feel you just can't handle the barest essentials of your life. Give the healing process time to work before you turn to antidepressants for the "quick fix." You might also investigate *Hypericum perforatum* (also known as St. John's Wort), an herb that has received much media attention since 1997. Harold H. Bloomfield, M.D., et al., have written a book entitled *Hypericum & Depression* (Prelude Press, Los Angeles, 1996) that presents many details about using this herb for treating depression.

Altered sleeping patterns should not be ignored. Do you go to sleep early because you're exhausted and then wake up at 2 A.M., unable to go back to sleep for three or more hours? When you finally return to sleep do you sleep so hard that you can't get up? Such a sleep disorder is probably related to depression, and if it doesn't pass within two or three months, your life would be a lot easier if you checked with an expert.

A natural supplement you might want to check out for sleep problems is *melatonin*. Melatonin is a hormone, naturally produced by the body, that works to restore normal sleep patterns and is available in health food stores in most states. Doses as low as one milligram have been reported to help prevent "owl eyes" from occurring at two or three in the morning.

As with all medications, you should check with a qualified health-care consultant before taking melatonin or *Hypericum*. In some cases they can cause allergic reactions or other unwanted effects. So always self-medicate with caution and get professional advice if you're in doubt about the product or the dosage.

Any discussion of depression requires mentioning *agitated depression.* This type is a bit more difficult to recognize—especially in men—because it doesn't look or feel like what we commonly think of as a depressed state. The agitated variety masquerades as restlessness, inability to sit still, irritability, rapid and/or pressurized repetitive speech, and involvement in dangerous and/or exciting high-risk behaviors. All of the foregoing provide a manic *illusion* of progress, activity, and busy-ness. You "couldn't be" depressed—but you are, and you have camouflaged that reality with intense, organized activity.

It's important to recognize depression. Managing it consciously is also important. A good technique is to understand that depression comes and goes—gets better and worse—in waves. Try talking to it when it's intense and you're really hurting: "Hi, you were here last week [month]; I recognize you. Whenever you're around, I feel bad. But I'm not you—I'm *watching* you, and I notice how poorly I feel about me and my environment when you're here."

Important: If, instead of recognizing your symptoms, you act them out, the next wave of depression will return with *greater* intensity. If you recognize your symptoms *as* symptoms of depression instead of reality, the intensity of each following wave of depression will *diminish.* Again, ask your coach-therapist about this technique.

ACCEPTANCE

The acceptance stage is pretty much what it sounds like—and getting to it is hard. Basically, it's your reward for going through hell. You have to maneuver in and out of denial, anger, bargaining, and depression a few times (and, again, not necessarily in that order) if you are to move into acceptance. Now and then you'll believe you're there, but you probably aren't—not quite. Pure and simple: it takes time. The arrival of acceptance is the moment—more often an increasing progression of moments—when the reality of your loss has found a place in your life.

You don't hate it anymore. You don't fight it anymore. It happened. It's so. *And* you will go on.

In the dictionary, "acceptance" is defined as "the act of taking or receiving something offered." Although you may not see it yet, you are being offered a new life.

Everyone thinks of changing the world,
but no one thinks of changing himself.
—Leo Tolstoy

2

PHOENIX RISING

INVENTING THE NEW YOU

Creation is always found in the company of destruction. Cycle after cycle, the two are inextricably woven together. There is an ancient myth of a splendid heron-like bird that sported red and gold plumage and had a life span of 500 years. When this magnificent bird, called "Phoenix" by the Greeks, came to the end of an allotted life span, it built and set ablaze its own funeral pyre, immolating itself. Afterward, it arose newborn from the ashes. With this myth, the Egyptians and Greeks taught the cycles of creation and destruction—that birth follows death, which follows birth, endlessly.

The Phoenix offers an enduring metaphor through which we can understand and honor the process of change that gives birth to new growth. We travel through cycles of creation and destruction daily, monthly, and yearly. After a deathlike sleep, we awaken each morning to a day just like the one that withered into midnight. Look around: everything in your life runs in cycles. Daily cycles of feeding, hygiene, moods, sex, and finance are contained within the larger cycles of months, seasons, and years.

21

A NEW BEGINNING

Fire seems cruel. It destroys everything in its path and plays no favorites. Yet in its power lies a paradox—it heralds a new cycle of creation. It prepares the ground—"hallows" it—for new growth. With death or divorce behind you, you have survived the fire. Precious portions of your heart were consumed, but your ground has been hallowed for a new beginning.

You can learn from the story of the Phoenix. Resting firmly on your accomplishments, you can feel the new you rising from the ashes. This new you can be better than any "you" before. You spent years growing up under the watchful eye of parents and teachers. If you're over thirty, you spent more years becoming who you are, watching for opportunities to improve yourself and your circumstances. And if you're over forty, you've also acquired wisdom and success that should be of great comfort to you now.

As the weeks and months pass, you find new energy awakening and taking form. If you learn from your experience, if you're willing to be open to the knowledge of others, you can make a new life, perhaps one that turns out even better than the one you've lost.

The fire is behind you now. Take your time dusting off the ashes. You'll need to get oriented, because you're going to re-imagine yourself. You're no longer that guy who got married and tried to live happily ever after. Success will follow more easily if you take whatever time you need to sort through your life before you embark on your new adventure. Nonetheless, sooner or later, you must embark.

As you move forward, keep in mind that everything you've accomplished has involved a learning curve—whether it was in sports, driving a car, using a computer, or developing your career. Relationships have learning curves as well. Among other things, we're going to explore ways to shorten that curve.

RESISTANCE AND AVOIDANCE

We are not always in control of our circumstances—only of how we handle them. Your recent loss illustrates the futility of trying to *control* your life when, at your human best, all you can do is control your *reac-*

tion to what's happening. Reality is what's happening to you now, and *your* reality is that you have a new adventure to grow into.

You probably know people who would rather die than change. They regard the unknown as too dangerous, threatening, or painful. They can't imagine that anything really good could come from change. So trapped in the status quo, they can't move on with their lives.

You say you want to wait a few years before you make changes? I say, you had a life once and you can have one again. Why wait? Time is not on your side. The time for action, the time to "just do it," is not as far off as you think. You can probably even feel the fear (excitement?) around the urge to grow again. Life is not to be wasted—this energy you feel stirring in you is yours to use, not to sit on.

Think of it this way: A terrific woman is waiting for you, and you're no good to her until *you're* ready. She is dependent upon your recovering your sense of worth and launching yourself into the process of finding her. She's out there now, waiting for you to heal your grief and return to the living.

What if you and Mrs. Right-for-You miss each other because you *don't* go into action? How will you feel if you miss her because you are afraid to saddle up and ride? While it is acceptable for modern women to be more assertive, your new lady is unlikely to canter up to your house, slip off her white horse, hang her hat on the saddle horn, and then shimmy on up to your door. Even if you wish that would happen, *you* still have to do the personal work that will make her glad she shimmied up—or she'll just shimmy on by. You can bet that waiting for someone else to make the first move will cost you many wonderful opportunities to be happy again.

If your wife died recently, you may be concerned about what your friends and business associates think about your dating. They may think you're being disrespectful to her if you don't wait at least a year. Unquestionably, that *was* the standard. But the present standard requires that you ask yourself what's best for *you*. The expectations of others may not be relevant to who you are. You may want to wait a year or more before you start dating or you may want to date after a month or two. Dating soon after the death of your wife can be considered a great compliment to her and to your marriage. Having once found a great love, you would naturally want to have it again. Or, if you went through a divorce, probably by the time the divorce is final, you will feel that you have been through most of the grieving process and are ready to date immediately, regardless of what your friends think.

So, loss by either death or divorce leaves you with an important decision. Unless you're thinking of entering a monastery, the operative question is: how do you recreate a meaningful, passionate life? The rules for being thrown from a horse might apply here. Dust yourself off and get back in the saddle as soon as you can.

GOING IT ALONE

In the meantime, you'll be riding solo for a while. It's a time for solitude and some loneliness until the new you is in place. You're still a whole person, but you're also a *new* person, and you're learning just who you are now, without your "other half." This is a time of trial and error, of refinement, and of readying yourself to meet and attract interesting new women.

One cure for loneliness is to recognize that your life still contains important areas in which you *can* function alone. Before you lost her, there were situations in which your wife's influence was minimal, such as your hobbies or perhaps your work. These and similar aspects of your life can provide structure right now. Use them to motivate and balance you, to provide you with a focus, to keep you company as you adjust to your aloneness and its effect on every part of your life.

Your goal is to maintain what's left of your family, friends, and work while you clarify your values, expand your horizons, improve your personal health, and develop a greater awareness of your internal workings.

For instance, what makes you happy? How do you find contentment? The very fact that you're reading this book, a book about getting your life going again, probably means you are a person with plenty of drive and initiative. If you have a problem, *you're* the first stage of the solution. You may be tempted just to dive in and start dating without thinking through a plan. That can work, but it tends to lead to bruises and scrapes.

I think of a child who's given his first bike. If no one teaches him, he's still going to get on that bike. Then he is going to crash and get up and keep crashing and keep getting up, over and over again, until he is riding like the wind. But how do the boy and the bike fare in the process? They suffer their share of cuts, road rash, bumps, dented fenders, twisted handlebars, bent pedals, and scuffed paint. Was there a better way? A parent, teacher, or coach with a strategy for success would have spared the boy and the bike a lot of grief.

My aim is to quiet your impatience and motivate you to develop your own personal strategy for something that's a lot more important than riding a bike. Once you have your own strategy, you'll trust it and you'll use it to discover your new lover and best friend.

FINDING YOUR OWN BEST SELF

By this time in your life you know a lot, but if you're interested in change and self-improvement, you'll want to be more aware of what you're expressing and more willing to confront what you *don't* know. This requires a spirit of adventure and a willingness to experiment. It's a widely recognized fact that what we *know* is not the problem. What we *don't* know is the problem, and that is what ends up defeating us. To be precise: it's time for expanding our own self-awareness.

Risk is now as important to you as the sun is to a sundial. Explore new dimensions of yourself. Neither you nor your new lady are likely to commit to a new relationship unless you are offered an improvement over what you had—both of you are hoping for more.

I want you to assume that interesting women are bored with men who, regardless of their age, haven't matured past their twenties. You and I have reached a certain level in our careers. We learned how to respond to the family and the life we *had*. And along the way we probably learned to expect that women would make the changes necessary to accommodate who *we* are. Let me assure you: women recognize this as a flaw. They also see it as callous and boring! More and more women are expecting partnership, a relationship that will make both lives work. The goal in a partnership is to help each other expand, to satisfy each person's hopes and desires in an environment of mutuality.

One of the changes most men need to make to achieve mutuality— to become a genuine partner—centers around the issue of being "right." Among the great sicknesses in the world is the belief that "because I thought it, it must be so—or I wouldn't have thought it." Whether we're discussing something over the kitchen sink or negotiating issues in the Middle East, we men are often addicted to being right.

In personal relationships, there is a big difference between winning and needing to be right. In the truest sense, winning involves both sides having a satisfactory outcome; being "right" does not. In relationships especially, you really do win when you both win—winning doesn't mean someone has to lose. As you embark on your new life, keep in mind that for *both* of you to win is more important than for you alone to be right. You can be right and appear to be the winner, but both you and your relationship are losing—and that's not okay.

This is important. If you're not clear about the concept of mutuality, find a coach, a trusted friend, or a weekend relationship seminar, and learn how to perfect the skills related to self-awareness and the "win-win" solution. You'll be surprised at how much you can learn through videos, books, and weekend workshops.

Self-awareness leads to genuine self-control and makes you easy— and more interesting—to be with. You cease to threaten others, you don't overreact, and you don't get inappropriately or disproportionately upset. And you will sense when control of your environment is important and when it's not.

All of this adds to your integrity. Listen: Integrity means you are who you say you are. Being who you say you are depends a lot on your being present and not being preoccupied. These important living skills make you *more*—more available, more approachable, more comfortable, and more safe to be around. In a word, they make you more interesting.

But while it's important to be an interesting person, it's equally important that you not be focused on yourself when you're with others. So the best way to be interesting is to be *interested*—interested in others. You detract from who you are if you persist in directing attention to how interesting *you* are. To build any relationship, it is vital that you be more interested in the other person than you are in yourself. To succeed in finding a new partner, you'll want to be self-aware without being self-involved.

And I'm not talking about being phony or manipulative—I'm talking about being "present-able" and real. The skillfulness with which we deliver ourselves is one of the ingredients for making a rich, sweet environment wherever we are. The quality of our actions as we do this depends upon the quality of the intentions behind them, which is why sincerity and interest matter. *The greater your self-knowledge, the greater your integrity—the greater your integrity, the greater your success.*

STOP LIVING ON AUTOMATIC

After a trauma like death or divorce, it's easy to lose track of what you're looking for in life. You can stumble through your days never knowing why you're acting the way you are. When you're not aware that you have and can make choices, you're living on automatic. You are carrying impulses or urges that you haven't really thought much about or prefer not to act out—yet you act them out anyway. These impulses may be whispers from the monkey mind, or they may be old habits you've wanted to kick. For instance, someone does or says something that causes you to overreact or to withdraw—in a way that you can't begin to explain. Your reaction is not one of choice, you are on automatic. Being on automatic deprives you of choice. It leaves you stuck in your ways, making it likely that you will fall back into an old behavior cycle from which you've tried to break free. Automatic is a dynamic that maintains old relationship patterns and plays old tapes that defeat your efforts to develop a better life.

Self-discovery is a must. The fact is that you, like the rest of us, are doomed to repeat your old patterns until *you* break them. You've seen others stay stuck in the same groove no matter how much they say they want to move on. They marry, get divorced, and marry right back into the same unlearned lesson. They've found a way to preserve the unhappy status quo by making the same old mistakes in brand new ways. For example, "She's not like my other two alcoholic wives. She's been in recovery for ninety days." (Funny, but I've heard it.) We humans are bound by a basic concept: learn, and we move on; don't, and we stagnate in the muck of the same old painful lessons. This sounds simple, but it's not simple to do. Humming the tune and dancing the dance are two very different skills.

Women are critical of men, not so much for any intellectual deficiency but for a lack of emotional and relationship savvy. How you acquire this savvy and pursue personal advancement depends a lot on your environment and who you are. For instance, what is your current emotional status? Your budget? Time available? Vocation? Are you near a city, or do you live in a small town? Your circumstances will determine how you approach educating your new self about relationships. In any case, it's time for the new "you-that-you-are-becoming" to give some consideration to the many self-discovery courses available in books, tapes, weekend seminars and other forums.

A popular definition of insanity is expecting different results from doing the same thing over and over. So read all you want, but until you *change your behavior* you remain snared by your old patterns.

The following resources are filled with behavior-changing insights, begging to be implemented. I consider them basic to any "suddenly single's" library. Don't be afraid to spend some time on this process. Remember the boy on the bicycle, and don't get too impatient. You are doing yourself—and your future mate—a great disservice if you skimp on this step as you develop the new you.

BOOKS

For you or a men's discussion group, I particularly recommend the following three books and suggest that they be studied together:

What Smart Women Know, by Steven Carter and Julia Sokol (M. Evans, 2000).
Men Who Can't Love, by Steven Carter and Julia Sokol (Berkley, 1997).
This is How Love Works, by Steven Carter (M. Evans, 2001).

The first two are written for women about menand contain break-through material for us to study. As we become aware of a woman's point of view and learn how she is affected by our patterns of thinking, feeling, and behaving, we recognize the need to soften—to be more insightful and responsive to her. And that leads to a big win for us! In the third book, Carter, writing alone, helps men solve the problems he and Sokol, writing together, describe in the first two books.

Men Are from Mars, Women Are from Venus: A Practical Guide for Improving Communication and Getting What You Want in Your Relationships, by John Gray, Ph.D. (HarperCollins, 1992). This immensely popular relationship counselor offers ways to identify, understand, and deal with the essential differences between men and women. He advises that you just accept these differences and quit expecting things to be otherwise.

Spiritual Divorce: Divorce as a Catalyst for an Extraordinary Life, by Debbie Ford (Harper San Francisco, 2001). This book presents the author's own story of healing after divorce. Her self-discovery tools and exercises offer the reader a pathway to change and to new beginnings. A valuable feature of this book is its explanation of how to release angry feelings caused by divorce.

Send Me Someone, by Diana von Welanetz Wentworth (Renaissance Books, 2001). A mystical, romantic, never-a-dull-moment memoir. As the author's husband of twenty-five years was dying, he promised he'd send her someone to love. When she met and married Ted Wentworth—author of the book you're now reading—she knew her late husband had kept his promise.

What Women Want Men to Know, by Barbara De Angelis, Ph.D. (Hyperion, 2001). This book is a useful guide for going deeper in your relationship—especially because it's not just a collection of theories. It's the result of a real, wide-reaching life experience. The author, a well-known authority on romantic relationships, sent out thousands of questionnaires, and the answers she received are the foundations of this book.

Secrets About Men Every Woman Should Know, by Barbara De Angelis, Ph.D. (Dell, 1991). Read this powerful book and learn how to talk to your lady about what you really want! You'll also open the door for her to discuss what she really wants.

Getting to "I Do," by Patricia Allen, Ph.D. (Avon Books, 1995). Ever wonder what your lovely lady talks about in the locker room? It's definitely not recipes, sewing tricks, and hairstyles. Here's your chance to eavesdrop on the female strategy. It lets you in on what *she* wants, and how *she* thinks, and what's on *her* mind.

Why Men Are the Way They Are, by Warren Farrell, Ph.D. (Berkley, 1990). With remarkable and original insights, cartoons, and extensive research, this book answers virtually every question women ask about men in a way that rings true for men.

Women Can't Hear What Men Don't Say, by Warren Farrell, Ph.D. (J.P. Tarcher, 2000). This book articulates what a man in a relationship feels but doesn't say. It is perfect for anyone who has difficulty handling personal criticism, or any couple struggling to communicate. Farrell's easy-to-read style, humor, and research make it easy to reexamine myths about men that lead to relationship problems.

The Dance of Connection: How to Talk to Someone When You're Mad, Hurt, Scared, Frustrated, Insulted, Betrayed, or Desperate, by Harriet Lerner, Ph.D. (HarperCollins, 2001). This best-selling author is a specialist in dealing with difficult relationships. She teaches strategies for dealing with various problems, such as revealing vulnerabilities, voicing complaints or concerns, apologizing, and setting limits.

Feal the Fear and Do It Anyway, by Susan Jeffers, Ph.D. (Fawcett, 1992). An excellent resource for freeing yourself from emotional prisons. This book helps you learn the life skills you need to overcome fear and be willing to love again. Fear is universal, says the author, but you can choose not to stay in bondage to it. She offers specific counsel on how to face fear and work through it. You *can* love again.

Dare to Connect: Reaching Out in Romance, Friendship, and the Workplace, by Susan Jeffers, Ph.D. (Fawcett, 1993). With specific strategies, the author helps you overcome feelings of anxiety, uncertainty, loneliness, isolation, and unworthiness and transform them into feelings of acceptance and belonging. Here is sound, practical advice on dealing with fears of intimacy and rejection.

The Way of the Superior Man: A Spiritual Guide to Mastering the Challenges of Women, Work, and Sexual Desire, by David Deida (Plexus, 1997). With honesty and insight, the author discusses many of the tough issues in men's lives. He emphasizes the concern over what it means to be a man in today's world and how a man can live with integrity and authenticity. This is a particularly useful book for men who did not grow up with good masculine role models.

You Just Don't Understand: Women and Men in Conversation, by Deborah Tannen (Quill, 2001). With rare combination of scientific and delightful, humorous writing, Tannen show why women and men can walk away from the same conversation with completely different impressions of what was said. Filled with lively and entertaining examples of real conversations, this book gives you the tools to understand what goes wrong and to find a common language you can use to strengthen all your relationships.

Body Language, by Julius Fast (Pocket, 1988). This book discusses how you can "read" other people by being aware of their body movements and posture. Knowing subtle ways that feeling are communicated by the physical body gives you useful information about others and also makes you more aware of what you may be unconsciously "saying" to someone.

A Conscious Person's Guide to Relationships, by Ken Keyes, Jr. (Living Love, 1979). Using his breakthrough concept of having preferences rather than needs, Keyes asks you to look more closely at emotional responses that are triggered when you don't get your own way. Much of the time, you probably respond automatically, not realizing you are making choices, and that turns your relationship into a roller coaster. Keyes's ideas help to smooth out the ride. (This simple, excellent book is out of print but well worth the trip to the library, your local used-book store, or a search of Internet resources.)

AUDIOTAPES

How to Love a Woman: On Intimacy and the Erotic Life of Women, by Clarissa Pinkola Estes (Sounds True, 1997). The best-selling author of *Women Who Run With the Wolves*, explains how women want and need to be treated. It includes the author's own list of twelve qualities to look for in a mate. Myths and stories clearly illustrate the ways in which love relationships challenge, nourish and transform both partners.

Hot Monogamy: Essential Steps to More Passionate, Intimate Lovemaking, by Pat Love, Ph.D. (Sounds True, 1994). The presenter, a sex therapist, offers her nine-step program—starting with a self-quiz for determining your sexual style so you can pinpoint areas you need to work on. Once problems are identified, Dr. Love assists you in making appropriate positive changes. Guidelines and resources for finding a sex therapist are also included.

Making Relationships Work, by Barbara De Angelis, Ph.D. (Hay House, 1995). This powerful audio program works at the most common reasons couples fight. It also teaches right and wrong ways to communicate, how to keep your partner in love and faithful, and strategies for avoiding the biggest mistakes that usually occur in relationships.

End the Struggle and Dance with Life: How to Build Yourself Up When the World Gets You Down," by Susan Jeffers, Ph.D. (Audio Renaissance, 1996). Here, the author of the extremely popular *Feel the Fear and Do It Anyway* gives common reasons for fearfulness and assists readers in identifying times when fear is motivating their behavior. Especially helpful are Jeffers's techniques for taking positive, proactive steps toward goals and flowing more easily with life's ups and downs.

VIDEOTAPES

The Human Sexes: A Natural History of Man and Woman, by Desmond Morris. Human behavior, including human sexuality and biology, is explained from the viewpoint of anthropology. The information presented here is both fascinating and revealing. Watch it to learn more about why we all tend to feel and act as we do. (Distributed by Discovery Channel Video. For more information, see http://shopping.discovery.com.)

Many other outstanding audio and videotapes are available today. The two companies I recommend are Nightingale-Conant at 1-800-525-9000 and Sounds True at 1-800-333-9185. They will be happy to send you their catalogs on request.

DON'T BE AFRAID TO LEARN

When we are confronted with useful new information, a natural human resistance tends to show up and evaporate in the following sequence:

1. "There is no such thing."
2. "Hmmm, there may be something there after all."
3. "Everybody should know that."

You can easily get stuck at number one and sacrifice your success, so I urge you to stay open to the possibilities before you.

Once you have read self-help books, listened to audio tapes, watched videos, and attended workshops, you'll have exciting concepts and tools for carving out a new you, a new adventure, and a new way of life. You'll know that you're more interesting and more self-aware, and you'll feel so confident of your relationship skills that you can easily and naturally direct your attention toward others. You'll be *interested* in who they are and what makes them tick. In relationships, that makes for success!

From now on, see everyone you meet and every experience you have as either *a lesson or your goal.* Maybe it's failure itself that delivers valuable information that will later lead you to success, or maybe it's the dream you've been working so hard for. Whether it's one or the other is shrouded in mystery. Be ready to engage, and be just as ready to let go and move on. *Discovering the truth about yourself will bring you what you're looking for.* If you want more *in* your life and *from* your life, that goal will require a greater you. You receive from your adventure only what you *bring to it.* So if an expansive life is your goal, you can expect rewarding changes if you do the work necessary to create them.

How Life Goes On

When you're interested in meeting someone new, what sort of woman will you look for? Will she be different—or the same as you're accustomed to? What's essential? What's negotiable? Section II consists of four easy chapters that offer specific suggestions for developing a clear understanding about the kind of lady you want in your life—her physical, emotional, *and* spiritual attributes—so you can have a good idea of where you really want to go.

Section II also solves another problem. How do you find her? To help you avoid searching randomly, this section gives you more than a plan. It also suggests places you might find her, including cyberspace. It continues by offering a simple yet amazingly effective strategy: *interview* lots of women before you date them. If someone's not right, quickly move on. If she seems promising, get ready for that next step.

You're older and wiser now, but dating is still a high-risk enterprise and rejection is part of the game. Your chances for success improve if, along with knowing what you want, you understand what women want and what appeals to them. What attitudes do women appreciate? What makes you attractive to them? What will you talk about? What do you want to *avoid* saying and doing? Here are valuable pointers.

"*My preference is for someone who's afraid of closeness, like me.*"

3

PLANNING THE WORK

WHAT'S YOUR DREAM?

Before you jump into dating, you'll want to develop a plan. You'll want to ask yourself some questions. For example, what do you really want in a woman—the one you'll ultimately be with? Or, you might want to start by naming the qualities that you would prefer *not* to re-experience. By making a list of negotiable and non-negotiable qualities that are important to you, you'll have a better chance for success.

Let's agree that the approach you used as a younger man is due for revision. You need new tools and new ways of thinking in order to present yourself as the mature man you are now.

Too many of us fall for a woman too quickly—or not at all—for lack of a plan. We don't know what we want, and we can't see beyond our sexual urges to take a closer look until it's too late. In this chapter I have taken a lifetime of information and organized it so you can use or discard it according to your current or anticipated needs.

Whether the plan is in your head or on paper doesn't matter. You can evaluate your goals and whether you need to make personal changes to meet those goals. Make your strategy honest and straightforward: plan the work—then work the plan.

Think of yourself as working on a jigsaw puzzle, and the missing piece you're looking for must fit—for *both* of you. Recognize ahead of time that not only are you going to find some crazies along the way, but *you're* going to play the role of Mr. Not-So-Right with a few women as well. In other words, you're going to be the jerk now and then. Don't take it personally. Your biggest hassles will be rejection, disappointment, and feelings of inadequacy. But if you understand that from the beginning, you can expect these discomforts. You will recognize that they, too, are part of the plan.

SELF-PORTRAIT VS. RÉSUMÉ

Let's define some terms. Every woman you date is going to lead with her self-portrait—what she wants to look like instead of who she really is. You also have a self-portrait, and you're going to do the same thing.

Her résumé—her true personal history, including her accomplishments *and* failures—is, like yours, another matter. If someone is genuine, the résumé lines up rather easily with the self-portrait. Should you detect discrepancies between the two, I advise you to look a little closer. For example, something is not quite "as advertised" about a woman who tells you how loving and loyal she is but has three broken marriages and no relationship with her children. Or, she might talk big but seem to have no history of actual accomplishment and no evidence of being able to maintain herself intelligently in the material world: she drives a ratty car, can't hold a job, and doesn't have a credit card. The same thing, by the way, applies to you.

Before you start dating, think about the qualities you are looking for in a partner. Following is a checklist that can help you evaluate her résumé. It will help you distinguish between what is necessary and what is negotiable.

HER PHYSICAL RÉSUMÉ

As men we notice a woman's physical attributes first. These include:

1. Attractiveness
2. Age
3. Health
4. Taste

Attractiveness. Does she have to be beautiful? If she happens to be beautiful, that's just a bonus to be balanced with her other attributes. Her being "lovely" might be more important than her being beautiful. To me, a lovely woman is one who has refined social skills and whose sweetness comes from the inside, from the heart. I looked for loveliness, because I wanted to learn from someone like that. I wanted to love who I was in her eyes, to be her hero, and to be playful with her for the rest of our lives.

Age. Is your new lady going to be your partner? Doesn't that mean that she must be in your age group, plus or minus eight years or so? When I started my search, I envisioned my new wife as five to ten years younger than me. She turned out to be only three years younger, and that was just fine.

Are you open to marrying a woman older than you are? If you found your true love and learned that she was five years older than you, would you tell her she was too old? If not, don't rule out the possibility that the perfect woman for you might be slightly older than you are. Your plan is only on paper—not cast in concrete. You made it to give you a start, and it's easy to change. Never forget your goal: You're looking for a rare and special fit, your life mate—aren't you?

On this note, we need to consider "the trophy"—a flashy woman who is probably a lot younger than you are. I'm not suggesting that trophies are out of the question, only that they're so risky you'd be wise to plan them *out* of your new life. That way, if one shows up, fitting her into your plan will be extra difficult, as it should be. Imagine: there you are at forty-five and she is twenty-three, two years younger than your youngest daughter—and you want to do *whaaaat?* And why is *she* interested?

39

The question is this: Do you want to be her partner and lover, or the father she never had? Would it bother you that she couldn't share your memories or music? (JFK is not a rock band.) As a couple it will be difficult to fit into each other's social circles—especially the ones you enjoyed before you lost your first wife. Couples connect with other couples. If you saw a couple walking toward you and you knew that the very young woman holding hands with the man wasn't his daughter, what would you think? ("Hey, hey, hey—lucky dog," is not the correct answer.)

Consider, also, your emotional comfort in years ahead. Marrying a much younger woman might be a short-term pleasure that carries long-term regret—for both of you. Twenty years' difference will be hard on her later on when you're seventy and she's only fifty. When you're eighty, the difference becomes overwhelming. Will you secretly worry that she wanted children and you failed to have them with her? Or do you see yourself having them, which means you'll be putting children through college when you're seventy-five? Do you worry that—Viagra notwithstanding—you might slow down sexually and, in the shadow of that, she might step outside the marriage? Even if she promises that it could never happen, would you be concerned that it might? How does that uneasiness affect you? How does it feel to know I'm not making this stuff up?

Health. How well does she take care of her health? We're all responsible for maintaining ourselves as best we can, so that as we grow older we don't become a physical or financial burden to ourselves or—worse—to our nearest and dearest. Still, we may take excellent care of ourselves and have serious illness strike anyway; at that point, you want to have the sincerity and grace to say, "It is my extreme pleasure to be with you through this."

I'm not a volunteer. Still, just as I wouldn't avoid my true love were she older, neither would I walk away from her if she were dealing with ill health or limitation. But feeling sorry for a person or having her need you or feel grateful to you is not the basis of a relationship—especially not an intimate one. Therefore, how she takes care of herself should matter to you.

Taste. There is, at times, a thin line between taste and manners. (See "Manners," page 44.) First of all, is how she dresses and what she chooses as an environment pleasing to you? Her taste needs to fit in—sufficiently—with yours so that you feel comfortable. There may be times when her sense of taste will fall more into the arena of manners and thus have an impact on the environment you share with her.

Accepting an invitation carries with it a responsibility to contribute to the party. For example, you don't wear a tux to a baseball game, and you don't wear jeans to the opera. All events have a theme. The ability to conceive a theme and carry it out is an art form. Overdressing or underdressing contaminates the theme of the event and thus can be regarded as both bad taste and bad manners. Although we now live in a kind of "anything goes" environment, and you may not place as much importance on this issue as I do, I urge you to notice her taste as it compares with yours. This may be more important than you think.

HER EMOTIONAL RÉSUMÉ

A woman's emotional résumé is less obvious but very important. It can help predict how she will treat you and the people around you and how the two of you, as a couple, will get along as your intimacy deepens. You will learn about her emotions through her behavior and moods rather than from her physical appearance. Emotions not only have a huge effect on relationships, they are the very essence of her ability to maintain an intimate relationship. So it is important that you seriously evaluate your lady in terms of the following:

1. Children
2. Parents
3. Social skills
4. Manners
5. Temperament/attitude
6. Friends
7. Safety
8. Fun
9. Self-esteem
10. Intimacy

Children. A woman's relationship with her children can tell you a lot about her. How do her kids respond to her? Do they seem to enjoy being with her or show signs of being uncomfortable? Does she speak well or poorly of them? And when they're dealing with their mom, what does their tone of voice and choice of words tell you about their feelings for her? If she has no relationship with them, why is that?

If she doesn't have children, that brings up a whole new emotional issue between you. How do you both feel about the patter of little feet? If she's childless and under forty, plan on having a second family. If you've had a vasectomy, plan on having it reversed.

The two of you may even agree that you won't have a family because *you've* already done that, and she understands that you don't want to do it again. But realize that you may have to renegotiate your agreement as you slowly but lovingly discover that she's in emotional pain without children and begins to work on you to understand that fact. This is not her fault. It's the way she's hard-wired. Nature makes you and me "wiggle" in definite ways and, as you know, men wiggle differently than women. Over time she may decide that you've been blessed by children and that *you're selfish* for depriving her of what you've had. After all, she'll say, what could be the problem with starting a family?

You know because you've done it. She doesn't know because she hasn't done it. If your experience with children was good, she's likely to want them all the more; if it wasn't, *you* may be more interested in a second chance to succeed now that you're older and wiser. Either way, if she's under forty, you're a strong prospect to participate in a growing family—again.

In any case, know where you need to draw the line for yourself. I like children. In my experience, children teach us to be less self-focused, they complete us, they deepen and mellow us. But I had two girls in college and *really* didn't want to start all over again. My hope was that if my new wife had children, the youngest would be older than ten. My strategy reflected my belief that marrying someone with children was less risky than marrying a woman with no children. But that was just a plan, nothing more. I knew when I found the right lady it wouldn't matter. Plans are made to be changed.

Parents. Her parents and siblings will also furnish clues to who she is emotionally. Let her know you're interested in her family of origin (and be willing to talk about your own). Encourage her to describe in detail what they're like, how they treated her, what was hurtful, and what the family did individually and together that was fun. What does she say about her current relationship with them?

Although meeting their daughter's new beau will usually cause parents to put their best self-portrait forward, you'll still be able to form important impressions about their effect on her early years. Are you welcomed, or are they "cordial" but disinterested—or rude? Does her previous account of her parents and her relationship with them seem accurate? It's a plus if you can all relax as you spend time together, but if your lady is a mature adult, parents will most likely be only marginal players in your life with her. They probably aren't deal breakers even if they are rude.

When you get to know the family, do you recognize any strange behavior in one or both of her parents? Heavy consumption of alcohol matters, as does obvious disrespect for one another. Anything a bit "crazy" in a parent is important. How has that trait affected your lady's life? Does she have it, too? We all bear a diluted version of our parents' "stuff." Maybe she's been working on minimizing its impact? Can you live with it regardless? Even if she's suppressing negative parental traits, they'll show up during the first year you're with her. Meeting the parents helps you spot the problem. If she's overcome it, you can value her all the more.

To a great extent, in-laws get a bad rap. Her parents love their child; they want to see her life work for her. They want her to be blessed with a good marriage, and they want to see her living with someone happily ever after. Your life will work better if you can get along with and even enjoy them. They're her parents, she loves them, and you can't speak against them—even if she agrees with you—without her harboring hard feelings toward you. Find the things you like about her family and focus on those qualities. Then, if you feel compelled to note that something is "off," *and* it's related to safety, health, or money, the two of you will be better able to talk about it. Any negative about her family that doesn't involve safety, health, or money isn't worth discussing. Period.

Social skills. How does she act around others? Is it different from how she acts when she is alone with you? How does she handle herself

43

around people she's just met? How does she handle herself around old friends of yours? How do people react to her? (They may see things you miss.) And how important is any of that to you? Is it important to you to have a partner who makes you look good in public? For example, you might occasionally be intimidated in a group, or just not be connecting in a social situation for some reason. Can she save the day?

Manners. We learn manners in order to avoid offending others with our conduct. Each of us has certain minimum standards of conduct that others must meet in order for us to feel comfortable with them. Table manners and language (including good grammar) are huge red flags and, like it or not, stratify us instantly. If either of you regards the other as coarse or ill-bred, the relationship is over on the first date.

A female friend of mine has a quick and easy test regarding others' table manners: Can they hold eating utensils correctly, lift the food to their face with reasonable skill, and chew with their mouths closed? If not, it's then fair to assume they have no intention of learning. Men, incidentally, fail this test far more often than women. Like it or not, manners do tell us a lot about a person—manners matter.

Temperament/Attitude. Temperament is an area in which opposites definitely do attract. If you're volatile, you're likely to be attracted by someone who is calm—and vice versa. If you are high-energy, aggressive, impatient, and competitive (the classic Type A personality) you will probably favor someone who is passive, relaxed, noncompetitive, and compliant (the classic Type B personality). Negative people tend to attract positive people who pass right over their negativity. But it's not always that way. Some fiery and passionate (or calm and collected) people need to be with partners much like themselves in order to feel understood and respected. What matters most is that you consider whether you will like being around someone with her temperament and attitude for the rest of your life. What looks exciting—or soothing—in the beginning may become exhausting or exasperating over time.

Friends. Because women see things men don't, another good check is to *watch* how her female friends respond to her. Simply listening to what those friends say isn't as reliable, because most women won't bad-mouth their friends in front of men. If women seem to love her and to be comfortable around her, you can feel more at ease.

For example, I dated "Miss X" for several months, and I really liked her, but something was "off." Small things were happening that I probably chose to ignore because parts of me were having a good time. One day as we were out shopping, she recognized a friend from her church. Miss X extended a very friendly greeting, opened her arms to the woman, and hugged her. Seeing this, I assumed they were old friends. I was amazed to see the other woman draw back in surprise and veiled distaste. The woman said, "Nice to see you," and made a quick exit. Miss X's friend had not only failed to reciprocate, she snubbed her openly in front of her male companion. *That woman knew something my blind spot kept me from seeing.*

We all have blind spots. Some are caused by failure to pay attention or inability to learn from experience, while others arise from insensitivity or lack of insight.

Safety. Most importantly, your relationship must feel emotionally safe to both of you. You must be able to tell each other whatever you want. You have to be able to be foolish and vulnerable in front of each other. How do you feel about yourself in her eyes? Are you able to let go of your image of yourself and just be you? Can you get beyond the mask you wear and surrender your self-portrait and fear of rejection? When each of you can feel safe with the other, you have a necessary piece of the foundation for a relationship, and you can build on that.

Fun. There are two obvious ways you can learn what she likes to do for fun. Asking her is good for conversation—it lets her know you're interested. And noticing what she enjoys will give you ideas beyond what she's told you. Like most people, she probably isn't aware of what she really likes to do. Also, ask her *when* she last did what she most likes to do. If she says "five years ago," you might wonder if she's any fun— or you might recognize that it would be really romantic to haul her off to do something fun that she hasn't done for a long while. If you're successful, that's hero stuff; she's looking for someone who can seize the moment to make her life more exciting in nice ways.

If what each of you likes to do doesn't match, remember it's okay to trade. You might say, "I'll go see your chick flick if you'll go to the races with me."

45

Self-esteem. Self-esteem basically refers to your reputation with yourself. How *is* your reputation with yourself? And how is hers with herself? If yours is good, and hers is good, you've got another chunk of the foundation for a rewarding relationship.

If your own self-esteem is poor, if you have a shaky ego and don't want a true partnership, you risk attracting a "bimbo." A bimbo is someone who clearly does not share your social or cultural values, accomplishments, virtues, or character. She also has low self-esteem and is therefore willing to overlook your blemishes and incompatibilities for the benefits you offer. You make a devil's bargain here: The reason a man doesn't want a smart, competent woman is because he fears being overwhelmed, submerged, or diminished. So he picks someone who will be attracted to his lesser virtues—like his money or his good looks—and who won't threaten him or try to change him. It's a bad trade. He won't get more than he brings to the relationship. If you have poor self-esteem, it takes more than a decision to change it. You have to go out and do something to make the change happen inside of you. Maybe it's time for a weekend self-esteem workshop. That's a step in the right direction—guaranteed.

Intimacy. Women commonly have a greater capacity for intimacy than men do. One reason is that men easily confuse sex with intimacy. Having been sexual, they assume they've been intimate. Therefore, they don't understand a woman's declared *need* for intimacy. However, as a man you can be sexual with many women and never be intimate with any of them. But if you've matured through certain life experiences, you've come to realize that everyone wants to feel known—to feel accepted, safe, loved, heard, and understood. You've learned that sharing those feelings promotes intimacy (into-me-see). Then, when the woman in your life looks deep into you, you'll love yourself even more as you see yourself reflected in her eyes. Now you're on your way to something wonderful.

HER SPIRITUAL RÉSUMÉ

Don't let the word "spiritual" put you off. Consider it synonymous with "inner nature" or "character." It encompasses:

1. Religion
2. Occupation
3. Accomplishments
4. Addictions/Vices
5. Sense of humor
6. Trust

Religion. As you get more serious with someone, religious feelings and values may be a source of agreement and shared satisfaction, or they may present an obstacle through which you, as a couple, must successfully maneuver in order to go on. Most of us formed our basic values as we were brought up, and we are either set or yielding with regard to them. Such values are very personal, and when everything is said and done, a couple's religious/spiritual values either do or do not fit together in some sort of reasonable way. Also, if one of you is devout and the other is not, this is similar to having different religious backgrounds. If the two of you have irreconcilable differences and you cannot compromise now, what will the next twenty years look like?

Occupation. In general, do you want someone who has a job, a career, or a life's work and all that it involves? Does she have to be financially successful, or do you care more that she believes in what she is doing and that the finances are not important?

Occupational compatibility is also an important issue. If one of you is on the road for weeks at a time, and that isn't comfortable for the one who remains behind, something is not going to work. Ditto for long commutes. Or if one of you has a career that requires a lot of socializing, and the other needs peace and solitude when he or she is away from work, what will this mean over the long haul? Or if you are in conflicting fields—one of you is, for example, a medical doctor and the other is a malpractice lawyer—will your professional passions create unavoidable difficulty in your personal life together? You can either not talk about what each of you does for a living, or you can recognize that your jobs are only one facet of yourselves.

Along similar lines: Could you marry a cop? Could you marry an executive of a Fortune 500 company? A college professor? Are you genuinely comfortable in the presence of a powerful woman? If not, why is she choosing you, and what do you have to offer her? Is there stuff you're not seeing, and does that mean you're turning into a bozo—the male equivalent of a bimbo?

Accomplishments. Here, in her spiritual résumé, we're looking beyond the generally recognized areas of accomplishment, such as career or financial success. Now we're talking about personal accomplishments: Is she a good friend? A good mother? Does she help others? Is she loyal? Can she be discreet? Does she maintain a decent credit rating (a character/responsibility issue)?

Suppose there is a large discrepancy between your respective financial accomplishments. Do you value another person's accomplishments even though they don't earn money? If you make more money than your partner does, she may see your contributions as having more value and inappropriately demean her own efforts and depreciate herself. How would you talk her out of this? And would you?

Addictions/Vices. Most people are now aware of the problems that accompany excessive drinking as well as other serious addictions. Addiction comes from trying to numb a spiritual emptiness rather than heal it. I decided I wouldn't risk venturing into a relationship with someone who was ruled by an addiction. Do you want to volunteer to support her vices or compulsions? That's what you will do if you try to "overlook" her drinking, drugging, overspending, or gambling because she's "so much fun" or "great in bed." She will soon require you to enable—to be her encouraging partner in—her addictions, and if you balk, she will more easily let go of you than her addictions. The best thing you can do for her is to walk away. Do it.

Sense of humor. This is a spiritual aspect of every person. We all think we have good taste and a good sense of humor. But, if you're observant, it's very obvious that people's self-perceptions are often inaccurate. Each of you must enjoy—or at least appreciate—the other's sense of humor. Only you can decide to spend the rest of your life with someone whose sense of humor is incompatible with yours. If she always wants to be "sincere" when you want to banter and "take it lightly," you'll need to decide if she has enough other good qualities for a trade-off in this area. Proceed with caution.

Trust. Trust is found in the presence of truth and integrity. Integrity means you are who you say you are. Both are essential components of being "real." What you do reflects your character—what you *do* is who you *are*. Over time, can you see that she is who she says she is, regardless of the circumstances? Does she, for example, keep her commitments to you and others; and, if she can't, is she willing to renegotiate them? If so, she is probably trustworthy. (Trust is further discussed in the context of distrust and character on page 90.)

If you cannot trust one another early on, the relationship will dissolve over a period of weeks or months as each of you withholds and withdraws from the other.

People who don't recognize the importance of truth, integrity, and trust, tend to have unfulfilling, shallow relationships that repeat themselves.

BUILDING FROM HERE

As I noted at the beginning of this chapter, building anything requires a plan, whether it's in your head or on paper. If you're going to build a wonderful house, there are certain minimums for success: laying out the floor plan, drawing the elevations, and noticing how it all conforms with how you like to live. While detailing the interior, you choose the qualities you *must* have, those you would like to have but are willing to do without, and you stay alert for those you absolutely can't tolerate. During construction you'll probably make changes—in yourself or in the house—regarding what you thought was important. And that's the way it is with serious relationships.

Regardless of how carefully we plan, we need to accept that perfection is not possible—and adapt. You will have what makes you happy if you're happy with what you have. So the bottom line is that you can plan in advance regarding issues that are essential to you, but plans are made to be changed. No one will fulfill every point on your checklist, and I'm sure you'll find that some items you once regarded as important will become trivial, and vice versa. Having made your decision, celebrate her goodness and overlook the small stuff—that's happiness.

THE GREEN

You don't want to find someone exactly like you. You're looking for someone who will complement your personality, someone who will blend with, not duplicate, who you are—intellectually, spiritually, sexually, socially, financially, and culturally.

I assume you have noticed how different you are with different women. It's as though they "color" who you are. Some bring out your worst traits, and you end up not liking yourself. With others, you're wonderful—better than you thought you could be. With some, you converse freely, sometimes about nothing in particular. With others, you're quiet and reserved and speak only rarely. Let me offer you a metaphor to help you understand this phenomenon, which is genuinely difficult to put into words.

Imagine that people are either blue or yellow. Think of yourself as blue and your partner as yellow. Then imagine your ideal relationship as a mixture of the two—a really rich shade of green. Neither one of you is "the green." The green has a life of its own and you create and experience it together. Being wonderfully lost in the green is like reading a good book or seeing an exciting movie—you're there, temporarily absorbed in the adventure to the exclusion of the rest of the world.

When you consistently like who *you* are with an important person in your life, thank the green. As the relationship develops, it begins to radiate its own unique shade of green, and both of you become absorbed in that third color. You experience no loss because you have created something beyond—and in addition to—both of you. When the relationship really clicks, you find yourselves in love with the green and longing to be with it. If your blue darkens or her yellow gets muddy, somehow the green changes; and when it gets discolored, it seems to affect your individual colors. If you don't take steps to restore its luster, you as a couple will wither and then invent excuses not to see one another. What you're looking for is a relationship where the two of you, together, can sustain that green.

Now let's get to the practical steps you can take to reach that goal.

"*So far, in purely visual terms, I like her.*"

*We must walk consciously only part way
toward our goal, and then leap in the
dark to our success.*
—*Henry David Thoreau*

4

WORKING THE PLAN

THE LESSON OR THE GOAL

Finally, it's time to work your plan. You can't avoid the challenges—you have to work your way *through* them. That means reading and taking self-discovery courses—and beginning to date. If your "givashitter" is busted you'll find that getting started is tough. I promise you, though, that the sooner you explore who you've become, the sooner the aliveness you crave will be yours.

You're looking for a woman you can love, someone you can give to, someone with whom you can expand your own capacity to love. *How* you care is who you *are*. Going shopping for someone to love *you* doesn't work. That turns you into a taker, which is not what you're about. You want to think of yourself—and to be—a man who is *offering* his love. You want the woman in your life to experience your caring as a deep, meaningful, sensitive gift, and to feel so safe emotionally that her heart can open and return an expanding love to you in even greater measure. *Your* role is to initiate that cycle. That's what successful men do.

The question is: How can you find someone to share all the love you have in you? With your giving spirit, with such a gift to bestow, you can be assured of making magic with the opportunities that come your way. The right woman could be someone you've known for ten years or the girl you loved once upon a time in high school. She might even be your neighbor or that stranger across the room. You can't tell until you fire up your courage and start the process of looking. That's your side of the equation.

You're most likely to find her through what I call "interviewing" and by dating lots of women. What's the difference between an interview and a date? Let's call it an interview when you're taking time to find out if you want to get to know someone. Coffee and a sweet roll in the morning before work might be an interview—ditto for a drink after work. It becomes a date when you ask her out with the intention of building a relationship—when you've decided you *do* want to know her better and you're focusing your attention on her through a more intimate lens.

You are not alone in your search, however. When you meet someone you're attracted to, she will most likely recognize your interest and anticipate your approach. If she's also interested, she will want to be absolutely graceful in matching your steps—as graceful as she'd be on a dance floor with you. If she doesn't seem interested, however, don't automatically assume that she would rather you go away. You don't know what's going on inside of her. So have enough caring, kindness, and persistence to step back a bit and let her sort things out for a week or so. Don't hover—give her some space.

If you're really interested and she seems equivocal or uninspired, it doesn't hurt to continue looking elsewhere as you quietly place your interest in her on the back burner. But be responsive and caring as you allow her a little time to know you before you give up. Never cling—or push. Once you've shown your interest, she may "pace" you for a short while, but it's still up to her to encourage you. Pacing is a woman's term that refers to the gradual incorporation of your influence into her life (as opposed to being "swept away" by you). If she plays too hard to get, your trying to force the connection will definitely not win the day. Move on—no blame. Her purpose in your life may have been just to teach you something that will prepare you for Mrs. Right-for-You.

Realize that everything works out for your good. Step back a minute, and you'll see the truth in that ancient concept. If she's not interested, that makes her one of the lessons and not the goal. Just say to yourself: "Whew, got that lesson behind me. What's next?" The answer to that question is very heartening: *Plenty* of women will be interested in you and who you are. You haven't failed. You've become better prepared for the next step in your adventure. Without these preparatory experiences you could never reach your goal.

Of course, once she makes it clear that she's not interested, just excuse yourself, put the rejection behind you and move on. Remember, you are looking for someone who will *cherish* your love.

My plan was that I would move on as soon as I realized the chemistry was not mutual. That meant both the woman and I had to notice the chemistry between us. If I liked her a lot and she felt nothing for me, it was time to be going.

In dating over a hundred women in two years, I learned—sometimes as early as on the first date—that about 10 percent of the women couldn't stand me. On the other hand, another 10 percent *loved* me.

Table 1: Partner Potential				
Disliked	**Bozo**	**So-So**	**Liked**	**Loved**
10%	20%	40%	20%	10%

Those were the extremes. Of the remaining 80 percent, the lower 20 percent thought I was a bozo, the 40 percent in the middle were just so-so about me, and the upper 20 percent liked me. (See Table 1.) You are likely to have similar percentages in your own experience. So what if some don't like you and others think you're a bozo. Shit happens! Let it go and move on. Persistence is the required virtue here. Keep trying. I think you'll also find that the top 30 percent of the women you meet are warm, wonderful, interesting, and interested. They deserve your taking time to carefully explore their potential while they explore yours. Yes, you're being interviewed too. Smart women have a "sorting strategy," and you should have one as well.

SORTING STRATEGY

In the thirty-plus age range, everyone has a résumé that's hard to hide. My own sorting strategy was to engage her in casual conversation about her feelings toward people and important events, how she dealt with challenges, and other significant parts of her life. At the same time, I had a very clear private agenda. I wanted to learn about her past because I believe that patterns from a person's past tend to project their future. Interested, easygoing discussion over the course of several dates revealed what I needed to know.

I now had her résumé. I had enough information to make a decision about whether to move on with the relationship. (She, no doubt, was doing the same thing.) Right from the first date I attempted to be honest, open, and forthcoming about myself. I told her what was easy for me, where I was clumsy, and what was hard for me that I avoided altogether. I didn't try to hide anything, because I wanted her to recognize early on whether we might fit. If she seemed shy or offered too little of herself, I'd move the conversation along by saying, "Tell me about yourself."

HOW IT WORKED FOR ME

The instant I found women who might qualify, or who might lead me to someone who might qualify, I sought "interviews" without delay. Some days I interviewed as many as two or three women. Two and a half years after I lost Sharon, I married interview number 131.

INTERVIEW TIPS

It's not important to keep track of how many women you have approached or how many you've dated. What *is* important is that your attitude is light and you provide an opportunity for conversation in a situation where the woman feels both physically and emotionally safe. Lunches, late afternoon coffee, or early dinners in a public place are all safe beginnings. (Important tip: Ask her to meet you there, so that, if she loses interest, she can depart—in her own car—when she wants to. How could she feel safer?)

If, at the end of an interview, you want to ask for a date, there are dozens of ways. One is simply to tell her that you'd like to see her again: "Next Friday would be good unless you have a better idea." When you ask her in a way that gives her some choice, you keep the lead as you concede that the decision is hers. She will appreciate you for that.

If she hesitates, that doesn't mean you're out. It means she is not quite sold. So continue to "close the sale" by offering conversation that helps her feel comfortable. You know how to do that—and if you don't, that's where the self-improvement courses are invaluable. Or, if you haven't taken courses yet, at least remember to play Ping-Pong with the conversation. Watch her—she probably has this skill. Back and forth keeps it interesting, engaging, and fun. Tell her a little bit about you, then ask her something about her. Easygoing conversation enables you to gather clues as to questions you can ask about her life and interests. Note something she's said that you're interested in and be curious. Ask her about it. Bring *her* out with gentle questions. If you don't do that, you're ignoring the art of conversation. When you talk only about yourself (in an attempt to be interesting instead of interested) you don't afford her an opportunity to talk about herself, and you are being a supreme boor. When you find a subject that interests *her*, develop it with her. She will love how she feels with you and value you for that feeling.

To monitor how you're doing, back off from time to time and notice if she's still interested. Does she let the conversation fade when you're quiet, or does she offer more of herself? If you're not selling well, *be sure you have your sense of humor ready.*

BODY LANGUAGE

Evidence that she's warming up to you will probably appear as more open, inviting, or vulnerable body language on her part. Her subconscious speaks the truth in small ways she's not even thinking about. You may notice her leaning toward you, uncrossing her arms, shaking her hair in a kind of preening motion, and showing greater interest in the conversation by asking about you. If you're walking with her, she may hold her purse so the hand closest to you is empty and available.

Even though she may remain outwardly distant or reserved, if her subconscious is encouraging you, then that's the truth about her. The ball is now in your court—follow up without delay by opening yourself more to her. Do or say something real to make her feel wonderful about herself. Notice her, as opposed to being self-absorbed or preoccupied with her response to you. Timing is everything. If you open and allow her to come in closer, she will match your moves—and you're off on an adventure. Again, avoid crowding her. Her feelings are part of the process. She can't respond until she is emotionally able.

If she leans back in her chair in a slouch or a sprawl, she's not interested yet. If she crosses her arms and turns one shoulder toward you, you're getting what's known as the cold shoulder. Worst of all, if she crosses her arms and legs, turns a shoulder, and leans back and squints—you're dead.

In any case, check her eyes. If you don't like what you see in them, she is simply another lesson. Excuse yourself with dignity and move on. (You can learn more about sexual body language from the Desmond Morris video series, *The Human Sexes, Volume 2*, "Language of the Sexes," distributed by Discovery Channel Video. For more information, go online at http://shopping.discovery.com.)

THE COMPUTER

Long ago in my business life I learned the value of remembering important details about people. Those details can be very important in future meetings. As I became more involved in dating, I developed a computer program to keep my interviewing and dating information straight as well. When I returned home from an interesting encounter, I would debrief myself by typing the important stuff into the computer in order to refresh my memory later. I was not comfortable seeing her again until I had reviewed my notes. In truth, I was meeting, interviewing, and dating lots of women, and I figured that if I got things crossed up, she wouldn't take me seriously, because she'd think I didn't care.

So, if I was interested in a woman who had a pet she obviously loved very much, I knew I'd better remember her pet's name. Far more important were such things as the names, ages, and genders of each of her children; where she had gone to school; and whether she was divorced or widowed (and if he died, the circumstances of his death). With this information—much to her surprise and delight—I could pick up the conversation where we left off. Doing whatever is necessary to remember important information is an honest key to working your plan well.

I want you to have a copy of my *Rate-a-Date* computer program. It's downloadable through www.spousetrap.net. The software covers the essentials you'll need to remember about the women you've met.

WHAT IS SHE WONDERING ABOUT YOU

Whether you think of the encounter as a brief interview-type situation or as a first date, don't forget that you're *both* trying to determine, as soon as possible, if spending more time together is going to be worthwhile.

Please remember this: A woman is looking for a man who will consistently, over time, intoxicate her with his affection. *Yes, affection—the non-sexual, physical and verbal expression of his deep caring for her.* Sex is usually the man's first thought, and while the woman may be very sexual, sex is pretty likely to be secondary to affection on her wish list. A woman's sexuality is most often genuinely engaged *after* she has opened her heart. Lust-at-first-sight may be charging the air between you, but lust isn't love—a deep, intimate friendship is necessary for love to blossom. Doesn't that make sense? Sex is important, but it can't—in either one of you—satisfy the emotional, psychological, and spiritual need for love.

She has dreams, too—she wants *more* out of life just like you do. She also wants to be held, nurtured, and protected. When a woman eventually sees that you are really *there*, that you have a capacity for intimacy, can comfort her fears, and are responsive to her needs, she'll become much more able to relax and be sexual with you. The sexual relationship that emerges when she realizes you are really *there* will be integrated with the love between you, and it will have a dimension and depth beyond mere recreation or release. And there, almost as an afterthought, is the magic you've *longed* for.

Look at this from another angle: as a mature, experienced man, you know that if a woman is being sexual with you but doesn't trust your love and caring, she is *using* sex, trading it for your companionship. She's either hoping to awaken love, intimacy, and caring in you, or she's using you as a sexual maintenance partner or a date she can count on until someone better shows up. If it is the latter, stay alert. You would not be the first man a woman dated for social contacts, professional advantage, money, or revenge on a former lover or mate. Regardless, if she's covertly using sex for a purpose—that's not part of your long-range goal.

When you meet someone who is genuinely interesting to you (and vice versa), you both begin—or at least begin to consider—working toward becoming a couple. The feelings are marvelous yet frightening, so this is not the time to ignore your better instincts. When you're together, you are continually sizing each other up. Are you the answer to her prayers? Is she the answer to yours? You're wondering, "Is she okay? Does she want to love or just to be loved? Can she give back as well as receive—or is she too needy?" *Naturally, she's also processing those questions about you.*

If she is for real, if she cares about you, she'll respond to you in proportion to your ability to make her feel physically and emotionally comfortable. She has no conscious control over when that will occur, because it happens on its own as her defenses soften. When an eye feels threatened, the eyelid shuts, and opening it is nearly impossible until the threat abates. The heart is that way, only more so. When the heart is no longer apprehensive, it slowly—very slowly—begins to open on its own. You can help her heart open to you by being loving and gentle with her as she ventures toward you. That heart-opening takes a while, so unless you can patiently care for her as it gradually unfolds, you have seen only her self-portrait.

How do you make a woman feel safe with the fact that you're interested in her? Forget what she can do for you—that's just your neediness. Pay attention to what you can do for her. Meet her feelings of reserve and caution by making your interest and appreciation of her known, and then don't crowd her; the next move is hers. Later, as you bumpily move toward each other, you can decide whether you can trust her with your emotions and your heart.

"Step a little closer, baby, and let some of the magic rub off."

5

ASKING FOR A DATE

WHAT ARE YOU REALLY ASKING FOR?

Asking for a date can be a high-risk adventure, especially if you have a low tolerance for rejection. This chapter offers a strategy that will almost certainly get you to a "yes." To appreciate this strategy, you must consider several factors.

ATTITUDE, ATTITUDE, ATTITUDE

You've learned that the person you were before you got married was a lot less mature than you are now. You have, in a sense, been through the wars. Now you're more experienced, you're capable of more, and you deserve more. The women you're interested in have probably been through a few wars by now too. That means what might have worked then won't work for you now. Today you should assume that women are experienced, and they wonder whether you can see them as anything more than a sex object—a sex toy. GIRLS ARE COOL, BOYS DROOL declares a California bumper sticker on a car driven by a pretty girl. What if we surprise them?

In your search, you can't assume that dating a woman entitles you to anything more than a "thank you" for your company. You're wise enough by now to be tactful and interested rather than aggressive or predatory. "How do I get somebody?" is no longer the question. The question now is, "How do I attract the right woman into my life?" When "How can I possess her?" is the thought running in the back of your head, your experience will be very different than if you're thinking, "I am really interested in her." If you're looking for quality, you don't want her to think your primary interest is a roll in the hay. If you're *not* looking for quality, why bother with a strategy?

In your work, you adopt an approach that offers service and reassurance. As you fulfill the customers' needs, you quiet their fears and give them hope for the future without emphasizing needs of your own. "Always stay in service" is a good business axiom, and it has a place in your personal life, too. When you approach a woman you're attracted to, start off with *her* in mind and watch her respond with *you* in mind. Offer her a part of yourself. If she treasures it, offer her more. And then more. You now have the maturity to realize that a giving relationship is infinitely more exciting and fulfilling than a taking relationship.

However, while business and social goals may be similar, the *skills* that work well in business can often crush the development of lasting relationships when used in a social setting. Our culture is concerned with how well men produce. When we succeed in the working world, we get a lot of bravos and material rewards, but the intense competition for success and advancement tends to sharpen our awareness in a way that leaves us oblivious to the subtle social skills we need in our personal lives.

There is a big difference between getting a product to market—with all of the attendant issues of authority and supervision—and nurturing a relationship to assure that both parties have their needs met. Knowing what a woman likes and dislikes, figuring out what makes her life work now and what will fulfill her wish list in the future might seem very unbusinesslike, but it's an outrageously successful strategy to get you what you want in a relationship.

FIRST IMPRESSIONS

The first time you admire a woman, you are visually attracted to some-one who is on another wavelength. With reference to the opposite sex, women define "interesting" differently than you and I do. You're prob-ably sexually attracted by her face, breasts, legs, and then maybe her overall figure, demeanor, and speech. From that, you judge how pretty and graceful she is. She, however, is going to note more than simply "Is he good-looking?" She is interested in you as an overall package and curious about whether you have your act together. Therefore, before you attract her attention, you want to be ready to be evaluated.

Male or female, first impressions do heavily influence our respons-es. She will notice your physical appearance and possibly be charmed, or even enchanted, by the quality of your response to her. She will sub-consciously measure your clothes (including your shoes), your groom-ing—how you take care of yourself—your character, attitude, gram-mar, disposition, manners, and etiquette for quality. Are you real? Do you appear to be a good person, a kind person, a safe person? Are you gracious? Do you have a good sense of humor? You'll do best if you are an interested man who has a sense of gentle humor and graciousness.

So be yourself and let her see that you're comfortable in your own skin, that you have a genuine initial appreciation of her, and that you'd like to talk with her. In other words, tether your sexuality to a tree for the time being.

MAKING CONVERSATION

The best opportunity to safely include a woman in your first moments together is to make casual conversation. You can do that almost any-where and out of almost anything—from standing in the rain and say-ing to a stranger, "Don't you just love ducks?" to "Something about this time of year makes me happy [or lazy or homesick or whatever]." Conversation can be as basic as "So where are you from?" or as quirky as "Don't you love elevators?" (if you meet her in an elevator). The main objective is to *open* a conversation—one that she can respond to and show interest in without seeming overly friendly. If she likes some-thing in your voice, she'll respond even if she doesn't like rain or ducks or elevators. You both know what's happening in the potential of the moment. Make it as easy, inviting, and non-threatening as you can.

I never found it easy to ask for a date; at times it was a very threatening experience. But once I learned how to open a conversation, I became much more spontaneous and natural even though I was executing a strategy, a plan that would take me where I wanted to go. Paradoxically, being spontaneous and natural sometimes calls for a strategy that you've worked out ahead of time. Everyone's delivery of an opener is different. Go with something that feels natural to you.

Your attitude is critical to your success—and essential to your delivery. What are you actually asking for? What do you really want? Are you just interested in her body? Doesn't that make you more interested in your needs than hers? Are you *engaging* her—or are you "hitting" on her? Hitting on a woman causes her to *react* to the hit. She becomes defensive and asks herself, "Should I give this guy any more ground?"

Instead, choose an approach that invites her to *respond* to you, that makes her feel like a winner. If you engage her with the intention of asking her out—because you're interested in her for herself—that gives her an opportunity to respond. In other words, you've included her. You've invited her in, rather than accosting her from outside.

She wants to be able to say to her friends, "I met this guy, we had a nice conversation, and I had a really good feeling about him. I was so pleased when he called and asked me out. I really like him." She wants a man with a wonderful, sexy energy that shines through him. But remember that for a woman, sex is the icing on the cake. You're the cake—*who* you are is the first thing she's interested in. Sex—the icing—is secondary. If she sees your approach as *primarily* sexy, she'll see you as needy and will presume that you're narrow and uninteresting. Her first impression will be one of not feeling safe or special at the very moment when you want her to feel interested and attracted to you.

What if she's wearing a wedding ring? She is probably married. But some available women will wear a ring to avoid being hit on by men—something like a "No Solicitors" sign. If you are deeply attracted, you can open with an innocent comment like the one about the ducks and the rain. When she responds, if you feel a connection, observe lightheartedly, "Is that a ring on your finger?" She'll say either "Yes—I'm married" or something like "No, I just wear it on that finger." If it's not really a wedding ring, you have the perfect conversation piece that may lead to her being interested.

THE BOOR

When you're socializing with her, remember to be more interested than interesting. Don't talk longer than two or three consecutive minutes, and always remember to maneuver your conversation back toward her with a question. If she's interested she'll pick up your question, run with it for a while, then pass it back. (*Women* know to do this.) If you go on for more than those two or three minutes, you are beginning to "hold forth." In her eyes, holding forth is likely to be a sign of an insensitive male—a self-focused boor. You don't like it when others monopolize the conversation, and neither does she.

FEMINISM—PERSONHOOD

Relationships between men and women have gone through big shifts in the past thirty years. The roles we've played and the ways in which we deal with and talk to one another have changed radically and will keep on changing for decades to come. The insightful man will regard feminism as the woman's cry for "personhood" rather than as an attack on men.

My current overview of these changes is that both sexes finally have permission to relax a bit, to treat each other more honestly and equally. But women are continuing to think differently about themselves and are making new rules about how they want to be treated. While that's good for them, men who don't know the new rules can make some colossal blunders.

There's an old cartoon image of a prehistoric guy going out with club in hand and dragging a lion back to his cave to feed the little woman who's kept the home fires burning. That image reflected the truth for thousands of years. A woman stayed at home to bear and raise her man's children and take care of his needs and desires. In many ways, a woman was seen (by women as well as men) as a *part* of the man, an extension of his mind, his heart, and his household—what was his was his, and what was hers was his. Men, in playing out this role, may have cared and provided for the women in their lives, but they didn't necessarily show respect for those women as *individuals* with a right to their own territory, their own place, their own "personhood" in the family and in the world.

I'LL CALL YOU (NOT!)

Here's an insight from women: Men are notorious for avoiding various combinations of "three little words"—such as "I love you" and "I can't dance." So why is it that "I'll call you" comes so quickly to their tongues at the end of a go-nowhere date? Men know they don't mean it when they say it, yet they say it because they think it's polite.

This is a woman's issue with men and in response to numerous requests, I agreed to air it here. When you say "I'll call you" and you don't, women tell me that it adds to your bullshit quotient and leads to your being categorized as a "jerk" with all the others who've said the same thing to her.

We men say "I'll call you" because we're trying to be polite. Instead we're being unkind. Women want a gracious ending to a date—not an untruthful one. If you would like to see her again, tell her so. If you know there was no real connection for you, why not be honest? If you can't tell her how things were for you, then be polite and say, "It was nice meeting you," or if you were introduced, say, "I will call Jane and thank her." You might say, "You are a very interesting person but you probably agree that we're not a romantic match." You could add, "It would be fun to stay in touch—maybe we can enjoy each other as friends." Or how about a little humor: "So, I know I'm on your frog list—and your feet don't quite fit my glass slippers—but would you keep me in mind for one of your girlfriends?"

Now that's half the discussion. The other is, they do the same thing to us. When you're sincerely telling her goodnight, saying you had a wonderful time and you'd like to call her again or see her next Friday, she also often lacks the nerve to poison the moment. Rather, she'll respond positively and later screen her phone calls when you call to follow up—driving *you* nuts. Whether it's the ladies or us doesn't matter. What does matter is that it's time to improve our skills.

There used to be an over-generalization that men were strong and women were weak; men were capable and women couldn't really fend for themselves; men were smart and women were . . . well . . . not as smart. As a result, men got into a rut.

These old habits make us seem condescending—even downright insulting—in our dealings with women. I urge you, instead, to think of each woman as "queen" of her own castle, sovereign of her own domain—meaning her life and experience. She is as important and as free as you are. *You would be smart to approach her with the respect that will earn you the right to be her partner.* If you're going to assume anything about her as a woman, assume that she is an expert about her own life and that she views life through a different window than you. She has the right to her own opinions, beliefs, loves, concerns, and preferences, just like you do. And she may or may not want to change some of those if the two of you click. There is a lot more to women than we have given them credit for. That's why the "Men's Movement" is still being invented. So until we men develop a fuller sense of ourselves and of women in general, we would be wise to embrace this concept: "When two *whole* people get together, the space between them is a lot more interesting."

"*Good morning. I'm Craig Nisbet, and I'm trying to meet women.*"

Think like a man of action and act like a man of thought.
—*Henri Bergson*

LOCATION, LOCATION, LOCATION

WHERE TO NOW?

Having the waiter at a nice restaurant or a friend at your office act as a go-between is quite different and much easier than having to summon the courage to approach a total stranger in a public park. Seeing someone in the library, meeting on the Internet, or encountering a person at a church function or in a social group are all very different experiences and call for you to scope out the situation in different ways.

"The library" is the term I use to describe any location that has a serious, formal, or uneasy atmosphere. Or a place where she has her head down, absorbed in something, or where there are lots of people who are quiet and focused. Examples include a church service, business meeting, therapist's waiting room where there are three or more people present, or even an airplane. If she doesn't respond to your approach in a place like that, your potential for humiliation is extreme. Opening a conversation with anyone, especially a member of the opposite sex, will draw everyone's attention to what's going on—and to how well you're progressing. In a "library" setting, especially if it's very public, there is no easy exit if you hit the wall.

When you're confronted with this type of situation, you would be better off waiting until she is up and moving. That will give you the chance to catch up and walk with her. When you are together walking down the steps from a building, you can easily make some comment about the building or where you've been—for example, "What would we do without libraries?" Or you can make a light comment on something you both observed: "That kid could really sneeze." If she responds, then the ball's in your court.

Where you make your move determines the extent of your potential for embarrassment. Your odds improve if you're especially alert to her frame of mind. Does she look busy and preoccupied, or relaxed and open? How much privacy do you have in this environment? If you get surprised or embarrassed after you approach her, can you retreat and exit gracefully?

Still, there are times when you must seize the moment or she will walk straight out of your life without ever knowing you were there. You are the only one who can decide what risks you're willing to take. In a safe setting, silly or inane comments can be engaging and inviting. "Sometimes I just have to say hello" will work if the environment is right. Consider this rule of thumb: The more private the setting, the more "inane" is okay.

Almost any store where your interests merge is an easy location—a bookstore, for example. It's still a public setting, but you're subject to less scrutiny, especially if you're both doing something together—say, perusing the shelves side by side. There, your opening remarks can carry an invitation for her to participate: "By any chance, do you know where . . . ?" or "Have you seen . . . ?" or "I'm looking for a book on Siamese cats . . . " or "I wish they'd print titles that are easier to read" or "Isn't it amazing how many books there are on this subject?"

What's easy for others might not be easy for you or me, and maybe that has to do with style. Instead of harshly comparing ourselves with others, it's better to relax and recognize that how someone else approaches a woman just might not be our style. We can all identify with the "library" problem, but even in that environment, what stops one guy and not another remains a mystery.

For instance, making "freeway friends"—connecting with someone while you're in traffic—would not be my style, but others tell me it's a great place to meet single women. While I found meeting in elevators exceptionally easy, others don't. In the elevator I sometimes spoke directly to the woman, at other times I offered my thought to the elevator doors. This was easier if fewer people were in the elevator. I would lean back, a little bored and tired, and watch the numbers click off. I'd start with, "Just can't have any more fun than this." That was a good opener for me. It was authentic, benign, humorous, and safe. The woman would usually respond to me or to the elevator door, but if she said anything, we would always alight from the elevator with a sense of connection and be able to continue our conversation for at least a few steps.

While you're walking, it's not difficult to add, "Do you come here often?" After that, you're on your own. Look around. Is there a coffee shop in the building or someplace very public and safe? Then you can say, "I think you're really nice" (though good delivery demands you truly feel what you're saying) or "I'm glad I said something—could I meet you tomorrow for a cup of coffee before work?"

"Could I meet you?" will leave her feeling less cornered than if you say "Would you meet me?" Each time you offer her the driver's seat, she will be attracted to fill that position—out of curiosity if nothing else. And that's how good things start.

SOME GOOD PLACES FOR CHANCE ENCOUNTERS

Morning coffee. Picture yourself at a high-end coffee store such as Peet's, Starbucks, or Diedrich's first thing in the morning. Nearly everyone is dressed for business and is therefore at his or her best.

Someone interests you and you make eye contact with her; if she holds that contact or does anything to encourage you, it's time to say hello. If she's alone, just make friendly conversation. For example, referring to your coffee and hers, you can say, "Good coffee. Have you tried their sandwiches?" Or "I come here every morning, but I don't think I've seen you here before" or "I'm new here. Is everything as good as their coffee?"

Lunch. You see an interesting-looking woman sitting alone at a table. Make eye contact while you're eating. If she acknowledges it, say something to her as you're leaving and walk slowly to allow her to respond. If she's reading, ask her what she is reading. Or you could say, "Do you always eat out?" or "Do you eat here often?" Those are good ways to find out if she'll be back so you can invite yourself to her table next time. Personally, if I encountered her a second time and she was friendly, I might ask her, "Would you like company at lunch tomorrow?" If she says, "Yes," you then make a date. Whether or not she shows for the lunch—the next move is hers.

Grocery store checkout line. The contents of her cart offer plenty of clues for you to open a conversation. Seeing several boxes of Kleenex, you might say, "Looks like maybe you've got that cold that's going around." Or if she buys the kind of jellybeans you like: "Aren't those the best? I swear they put something in them that makes me want another handful." Or if she has a magazine that you read often: "Did you see the article about _____ in the last issue?"

Anywhere—the light approach. If she's a total stranger, give her a shy look and offer, "My daughter says I should just say hello to you. Do you think she's right?" Such a beautifully inventive, nervy opening should engage her, but you always run the risk of "stepping in it." If she says "no" or dismisses you, it's not a disaster. She might be the loner of the century and have every reason never to want your floppy body in her life. Maybe you remind her of the father she hates. Nevertheless, just do it—approach her. And be sensitive to whatever fences she has around her territory.

If she's with a friend. The examples above presume that the woman is alone. If she's with another woman, you'll have to make quick decisions and face a bigger risk. First of all, you risk breaking into the "domain" the two of them have created. For example, she might be sitting with her best friend, who's been out of the country for the past five years, or who just broke up with a boyfriend, or any number of possibilities that would make you the "intruder" if you approach her.

You also run the risk of insulting the girlfriend, since, between the two women, you've "selected" one and "rejected" the other, and that can make the one you're interested in feel both complimented *and* very uncomfortable. As a result, she may make *you* feel uncomfortable for putting her in that awkward position.

If you decide to approach her, have the good sense to bring your manners with you. Acknowledge and include her friend in your greeting. Look at each of them and say hello to both of them before you turn your attention to the one who interests you.

I'm not trying to discourage you from approaching her if she's with a friend; I'm just reminding you to be ready with a careful, polite, inclusive approach. Delivery—saying what you have to say in an engaging way—is everything! If you're up for the moment, go for it— and have a graceful retreat in mind if you've blundered.

Referrals from friends. I announced to all my friends that I was dating again. All of the suddenly single men I know did the same thing. And while it works, it's not my favorite resource. I met some lovely women that way, but I was occasionally surprised by who my friends thought might be "just right" for me. In those instances, I felt no need to report back to them with any details other than to say, "Thank you, and keep looking."

Other good venues. Lectures and courses at such places as university extension seminars and art and photography classes are great places to meet like-minded women. Don't forget weekend self-discovery and relationship workshops and churches or temples. Do you have a hobby or particular interest? Have you always wanted to explore something? Follow that—she may be there. You love the outdoors? Check out the Sierra Club or a local camera club or birding group. Use your imagination. Women have broad interests—from scuba diving to rock climbing. Do you see yourself in any of those pictures?

Look through your local Sunday paper. Most have a page or even a whole section listing all sorts of local activities for the coming week. Think about organizations devoted to a purpose or cause, such as the Sierra Club, the Chamber of Commerce, charities, and drama or theater groups. Bookstores usually have book clubs, which are attended almost exclusively by *women.* These kinds of venues, if they contain your age group, are the opposite of awkward, since you automatically share common interests and have plenty of food for conversation.

Regardless of where you eventually meet someone, when you begin dating her seriously, you will soon have plenty to talk about.

ELECTRONIC ENCOUNTERS OF THE FIRST KIND

Just as women's self-image has grown and evolved through the years, so also has the entire world of dating. Today, more and more singles are using the Internet to find meaningful, high-quality connections that can lead to long-term or even lifetime relationships. In fact, cyberspace offers virtually worldwide opportunities to meet a Mrs.-Right-For-You.

Meeting people.com. Web sites offering state-of-the-art personal ads are proliferating on the Net—and for good reason. Imagine the possibility of "meeting" dozens of women in just one evening by studying profiles of their tastes, their values, and who they say they are. Most of the time you will also have photos to help you.

How exactly do these Web sites work? Generally, you have two options for finding interesting ladies: you can join a dating site or just browse. If you join, which usually requires that you supply a credit-card number and your e-mail address, you will be able to participate fully in the activities of the site. That ordinarily means posting your own personal information there, so interested women can contact you. Posting information about yourself involves answering various introductory questions that will form the basis of your "profile." The site may ask you for—and if you're serious you should include—a photograph of yourself. (Profiles with photos are browsed three times more often than profiles that leave women guessing, and for obvious reasons.) Expect your credit card to be charged either the nominal monthly charge or a flat annual rate.

If you just browse a site, you simply answer a few questions about the qualities you're looking for in a woman. You can narrow the search by geographical location, age range, religious preference, character traits, taste in music, or other qualities you feel are important. Once you hit "Enter," you will get a list of women whose profiles are a close match to the categories you have identified. After reading the profiles, you can e-mail the women who interest you.

A hit for a miss. With experience, you will become adept at clarifying your requests, since the number of "hits" you get depends upon how well you've refined your categories. It's best if the words in your search match what the ladies have written in their profiles. For instance, if you've queried for a "sense of humor," you'll miss the lady who says she "enjoys good jokes" or "likes to laugh." Or if you query for someone who is "physically fit," you will miss the woman who says, "I am in good shape" or "I take good care of myself." Learn the language of the site by reviewing some twenty-five or more profiles to develop a sense of the commonly accepted jargon and the keywords used to describe various qualities, interests, and behaviors. (So if they say "humor" make sure *you* say "humor.")

When searching, use your keyword and add on all its synonyms, related activities, or behaviors. If you want someone "spiritual," meaning someone who goes to church, you have to spell that out, because there is a distinction between "spiritual" (individual relationship with the Divine) and "religious" (relationship with the Divine through a group or organization). Describe what you want in as many words as you can.

You can find interest-specific sites based on religion, age range, lifestyle, sexual preference, and more. Remember, the World Wide Web is *literally* worldwide. If you fantasize about meeting a lovely Parisian, here's a way to do it anytime from the comfort of your own living room—no bars, no alcohol, no 2 A.M. breakfasts.

E = meet and connect. Once you send your e-mail responses and the replies come through, it's time to get real. An exaggerated cyber-portrait is all too easy to fabricate—even unintentionally. Men tend to stretch their heights and incomes, and women are inclined to fib about their ages and weights. When you're exchanging e-personals, one good policy is always to ask for another photograph—specifically a *recent* photograph—to be sure she hasn't led with an old one. Having her profile is just a first contact. She is still leading (as are you) with her cyber-portrait, so all she has to do is type in what she thinks you want to hear. Begin to qualify her. Develop the information that will make up her résumé by asking questions about her past—her interests, accomplishments, and experiences.

You'll find your true princess by taking time to weed out the cyber-frogs—and time is exactly what e-personals offer. As in a nineteenth-

77

century parlor where a couple positioned themselves at opposite ends of a settee for "idle conversation," e-mailing affords the opportunity for talking without touching. Allowing a longer period for mutual discovery is often a good investment; it builds friendship and intimacy, which makes relationships more meaningful and exciting in the long run. By exploring her thoughts and ideas first, you will create a deeper bond with a woman—remember friendship (meaning real connection) is her initial priority. The cyber-friendship you build tends to relax your preconditioned bias toward physical appearance. Your options increase greatly when you're enjoying who she is and are not totally driven by her unearthly beauty or what she "should" look like.

Tit for tat. Now, what about *your* cyber-portrait? While you're concerned about the authenticity of what she's presenting, she's trying to learn the truth about your self-portrait. Have you taken undue advantage of the impersonal nature of e-mail? Have you touched up your self-portrait? Is it more pretense than truth? You're far better off simply projecting yourself as a relaxed, confident man, offering honest information—and being who you are in the moment. If you hide out, you're wasting your own valuable time. (Likewise, don't attempt to be *under*whelming. Making yourself look like too little is no better than the opposite.)

Just be as accurate about your profile information as possible. You have the luxury of choosing your words carefully and reviewing them before you send the e-mail, so take full advantage of that. It's especially good if you are shy, like to think before you speak, or just tend to be tongue-tied meeting new women.

Don't take it personally. There is safety online—a "net" in the Net. Your e-mail exchanges can begin with an assumed screen name, knowing you will never meet one another unless you both agree. Your "commitment" at this point is extremely tentative. You can bare your soul in pixels, without having exchanged any deep, loving looks or touches to make "goodbye" more difficult. Rejection isn't as devastating, because it's less personal and so common. Don't expect your e-mail connections to continue beyond the first couple of exchanges. Most will fade into the sunset, a few may grow into friendships, and fewer still will mature into your wanting to meet in person. (Here's where the lovely Parisian may be "geographically undesirable.")

Getting personal. As your cyber-relationship becomes more comfortable, you can offer to exchange phone numbers. If she's interested, she'll be happy to do so. Read between the lines: If she seems reluctant, it may be time to move on. After you've had a few phone conversations, both of you will know if you want to meet face to face. It's appropriate for either one of you to take the lead here.

No guarantees. The Net has many computer-dating sites. You'll even find XmeetsY.com, a site that lists and indexes other dating sites and their areas of emphasis. All the sites are inexpensive, convenient, accessible, and probably "safe"—but the Net is constantly changing, so it's good policy to "let the buyer beware." No site can guarantee that the two of you will click when you meet. On the other hand, some psychologists suggest that if you build a deep enough bond through e-mailing and phone calls, only a total absence of chemistry will prevent you from falling in love when you meet. So watch out!

Where to go. You can find almost anything on the Net by using a search engine. If you use this approach, be warned in advance! You're almost certain to find yourself presented with X-rated Web sites by the multiple dozens. They are not only distracting, but they can also be the greatest time-wasters you will ever come across. A better approach may be to look at various sites that come to you through trusted sources. Keeping in mind that Web sites are constantly changing, some examples follow:

- Match.com
- Matchmaker.com
- Webcenter.love.aol.com
- Friendfinder.com
- Personals.Yahoo.com
- Relationships.com
- One-and-Only.com
- Jdate.com (Jewish singles)
- Jewishmatch.com
- LSingles.com (Mormon singles)
- Countrysingles.com (rural lifestyle)

REASONS TO AVOID CYBERSPACE

The Net, as wonderful as it is for seeking a mate, may be totally wrong for you. Among the possible reasons:

• You have good reason to maintain strict control of your privacy.
   a. What if you're prominent, newsworthy or a medium- to high-profile professional whose behavior is subject to scrutiny?
   b. Can you risk having an innocent interaction misinterpreted? Are you ready to become news or the object of gossip among your professional peers?
   c. What if you have money—lots of it—which means that weeding out gold-diggers is a must?
   d. Are you a physician, psychologist, or lawyer who can't risk connecting with a patient or client?
• In your business or profession, you would be inundated with husband-seekers for all the wrong reasons if you went public with your search for a mate.
• You have six children and feel you don't stand a chance in the open market.
• You have a disability, and you feel it's impossible to compete with Mr. Abs.
• You believe the marketplace of eligible women expects something you simply don't have.

OTHER OPTIONS

If browsing and a lack of personal contact just don't suit your style, two other avenues are available for you to try—the personal party and the matchmaker.

Party time. There are responsible groups that arrange private parties for singles, either at someone's home or at a rented location, usually a restaurant. Guests are screened to be sure the people who are invited are of like economic, educational, and social background, and admittance is by referral or sponsorship only. These parties are not openly advertised, so you must ask around to learn about those being held in your area. Such gatherings include dinner and dancing; they're upscale and carry a moderate cover charge. If you are comfortable meeting new people in a party setting, this presents an obvious opportunity.

EXECUTIVE DATING

Alternative approach. So, for whatever reason, you've decided computer dating isn't for you. Not to worry. There is a good alternative approach available: executive dating—private and dignified. But because it tends to be pricey, people in certain executive-level categories are more likely than others to be attracted to it.

Fits your needs. The clients of an executive dating service are usually mid- to high-profile professional men and women. As a client you submit to screening, pay a membership fee, and the confidential service prescreens potential matches for you.

Unmasking. After you become a member, your service coordinator will guide you through a personal interview, which may be videotaped and edited for viewing by prospective matches. You will also take personality tests. Yes, tests! The service needs to penetrate a possible "Sunday school" self-portrait and see the man you really are. Their job is to find your quirks and pet peeves and match them to those of a woman who won't be bothered by those idiosyncrasies. So this is the time to come clean about everything. Remember, you're looking for a keeper, not a player—tell the truth. Don't say you love opera, chess, and the theater if you don't. Hiring an executive dating service is a real commitment, one that requires a substantial investment of your money and time to give the service the greatest opportunity for success.

May I introduce you? After prescreening, you will be presented with one or more choices—in one or more different ways. You might view videotapes, read written personal greetings, or have a personal consultation with your coordinator about the candidates. At that point, the ball is back in your court. You decide who you want to contact.

Since the names you're given have an above-average chance of being a good fit, you should feel safe, comfortable, and secure in making the connections the staff members at the service recommend. They can't guarantee they've found Mrs. Right-For-You, but they can afford you the comfort of knowing these ladies are closer to what you're looking for and are worthy of your courteous and respectful attention.

81

GETTING SERIOUS ABOUT A RELATIONSHIP

Developing a significant relationship with a woman is exciting and rewarding when it's going well. But how do you handle it when great beginnings run amok? Who's at fault? Is one of you sabotaging things—and if so, what does that mean? Do you share unrealistic expectations? Or, sadly, do you really just not get along with each other? Section III looks at problems that may surface as your relationship deepens.

First, this section lays bare several little discussed areas of real life, the kind you wish your dad had told you about early on. They include such issues as office romance, the possibility of sexually transmitted disease, infidelity, fighting, and how to break up—along with suggestions about handling them gracefully.

Next, Section III examines certain serious emotional problems that could become apparent as the relationship evolves. What are the warning signs? What can you do? Assuming the problem lurks below the surface, how do you spot it? You'll find out how to equip yourself now with knowledge about "psychological landmines." In the future, you may be glad you did.

You'll also learn that many couples strengthen their relationship by securing feedback from skilled, trained observers—couples coaches, counselors, mediators—not necessarily because they are in trouble, but because they simply want the benefit of a different perspective to assist them in their development, individually and as a couple.

Section III is packed full of great stuff. You'll love it!

"Actually, I'm seeking a meaningless relationship."

Too often the opportunity knocks, but by the time you push back the chain, push back the bolt, unhook the two locks, and shut off the burglar alarm, it's too late.
—Rita Coolidge

7

ARE WE SERIOUS YET?

DEVELOPING YOUR RELATIONSHIP

Once you've found a woman you really enjoy being with, you'll want to avoid shooting yourself in the foot. The less time and experience—the less "history"—you have together, the more easily the relationship can be damaged. Remember the "green," and how it gets muddied when something is "off" between you? At the outset, both of you are going to be confronted with new values, feelings, and options that will occasionally discolor the green, no matter what. Most successful relationships get easier the longer the couple has been together. So, at least initially, stay open to the challenge when feelings in the relationship shift. And count on it: *shift happens.*

Be patient, loving, and learn the difference between responding and reacting. If either of you continually reacts and becomes defensive, self-referential,* or needy—as opposed to consistently responding by being "enough," generous, thoughtful, patient, and romantic—when things happen, you both have choices. You can let the incidents pass, or you can purposefully find ways to beautify the green. This is one of the times your coach can be very helpful.

If, together, you're unable to let the incidents pass, you as an individual now have important new information. You also have some decisions to make. Consider your history together. Based on the past, what does the future look like? "Better and better"? Or more of the "same old stuff"? Is the relationship worth an ongoing investment of your time and emotions, or is it time for an entirely different adventure? If it's time to move on, chalk it up to destiny—you've had another lesson.

In the old days, when something was "off" in a relationship, I usually regarded myself as a "victim" because, as anyone could see, I was perfect. (Feels that way to you, too, doesn't it?) In actuality, I was just as likely to be wrong as she was. Maybe I was the one who was muddying the green, and that, in turn, was affecting her. Any change in the green makes for differences in the two of us. When I'm off, I change the green for the worse, and that, in turn, negatively affects my partner. Look at the dynamics here. Most of the time the entire matter of faultfinding is irrelevant. The fact is that when the green's muddy, both of us are affected, and both have to contribute to the solution. And that requires skill.

You're not an expert in relationships, and "off" is a common problem. You rely on outside help for cars, computers, and plumbing, so why not for cultivation of the green? Again, we always feel it's the other person who needs help, but that's a sign that we may have missed something—a sign that we need to turn ourselves in for inspection and adjustment.

I sincerely urge you to invest in a weekly or bimonthly huddle with your coach. It's especially important when you're struggling with new and important relationships. Again, I refer you to chapter 11, "The Therapist as a Resource: For Me or for Us." During this dynamic, exploratory period, in which many worthy couples needlessly fall

---

*Example of self-referential behavior:
>   Little boy at door: "Can Jimmy come out to play?"
>   Mother: "No. Jimmy is very sick today."
>   Little boy: (Instead of being concerned about his friend) "Can I play with his toys?"

apart, I believe the insight and counsel of a couples coach can greatly reduce the risk of failure.

SABOTAGE

Have you ever suddenly found yourself on the outside of a great and growing relationship and wondered what happened? Have you ever watched yourself go full-tilt into a fight that erupted over seemingly nothing? That's how sabotage—the subconscious destruction of a relationship—feels. If a guy leaves work early, stops at a bar and gets drunk on his way home, and misses the much-anticipated family party celebrating his wedding anniversary—that's sabotage. The spiraling down of his relationship follows.

If you can learn to recognize your own capacity for sabotage, you may not eradicate it from your life, but you will greatly reduce the risk of unwittingly depriving yourself of the best that's yet to come. The following four insights will give you greater understanding of the sabotage issue:

1. Think of the quality and intensity of your life as your "field of action." We each have a field of action, and function within a "comfort zone" in that field.

    When life gets "too good," many of us tend to subconsciously sabotage our happiness and spiral down the ladder of success until we hit bottom—the floor of our comfort zone. Once there, we hear ourselves say, "That's enough! I've had it with this!" We realize deep inside that we can't (won't) tolerate any further discomfort or pain. That revelation stimulates action, sabotage ceases, and we experience relief as we climb back up through our comfort zone to the top where the cycle begins again.

    It's hard to imagine "too much" good, because not only do we strive to achieve rewards, we also believe that we are accepting and deserving of any and all goodies and entitlements that come along. So just how *do* we recognize when we're about to shoot ourselves in the foot? Do you feel guilty about your advantageous circumstances when you're with other people? Do you hear your monkey mind saying, "Boy! Things are really great—but what if I lost it all?" That's how you think and feel when you're hitting the ceiling of your comfort zone. Those thoughts and feelings can sweep you into a storm of *sub*conscious "resistance and avoidance" that will sabotage the success you've achieved. This happens in relationships as predictably as it does in our work and other aspects of our lives.

2. Another subconscious activator of sabotage is fear of loss. *Fear* of loss actually causes more damage than loss itself. When you lost your wife to death or divorce, you endured tremendous emotional and psychological pain. If she died, you have all the more reason to feel that you're a victim of circumstance. Therefore, it's even harder to open yourself to something new and wonderful again, since that, too, might be torn from your grasp. *Your subconscious fear of re-experiencing the intense emotional pain of another loss is a powerful saboteur, a powerful destroyer of incoming goodness.* Such fear can increase your tolerance for the "sour" elements of life, because the sweet ones are just too risky.

3. The third area of sabotage lies in the concept of sweet and sour. Imagine life in our comfort zone as a mix of sweet and sour. Each of us has a different tolerance for sweet and sour in some ratio of one to the other, and that ratio is constantly being calibrated inside us. When things get too sweet, we sabotage by engaging in conduct that generates sour. Some people live with a ratio of 70 percent sour and 30 percent sweet, but they may interact with others who are comfortable with no more than 30 percent sour and 70 percent sweet. Over time, this will generate some difficulties.

   For example, suppose *you* feel content when your life is composed of 70 percent sweet and 30 percent sour. You like your days to go pretty smoothly, but to keep them from getting too smooth, you get a charge out of mixing things up a bit, being challenged, jumping hurdles, and breaking rules. Your partner might look at that and see a formula for misery because she wants her life to be no less than 90 percent sweet and no more than 10 percent sour; otherwise she's cranky and feels exhausted all the time. In order to share a balanced relationship, you might have to learn to tolerate another 15 percent sweet in your life. In order to have a good, realistic, grounded relationship with another human being, she may need to tolerate another 10 percent sour in hers. This is how most successful couples subconsciously balance the potential for sabotage in their relationship.

Consider this: You could find yourself in a relationship so wonderful that it brings into your life 10 to 20 percent more sweetness than you've previously been able to tolerate. You might very well initiate the sabotage so that you can reduce the sweetness and get back to where you feel less threatened and more right—*more* like "yourself." In order to do this, in order to recapture the lost 10 to 20 percent sour and reduce the sweetness, you could start a fight, forget a birthday, be two hours late for something, and so on. That's sabotage.

To hold on to someone new and important in your life, it's essential that you have a sense of what your zone feels like so you can catch yourself before *you* sabotage what is becoming a fabulous relationship. If your partner is the one who's stirring up trouble in paradise, your lack of reaction to what she's doing will let it blow over. Be loving and present and supportive, as this is not the time to point out what's happening or how right and smart you are for spotting it. When the moment has completely passed, then and only then can the two of you explore whether or not what happened was sabotage. If you aren't aware of this ratio business and its place as part of your personal *comfort* zone, you can go through a lot of trials and make a lot of errors trying to adjust to one another's behavior.

Sweet and sour comfort zones mixed in with differences in our cultural, social, and economic backgrounds make life a little tricky.

4. With couples, the first person to "see the altar" may sabotage the relationship because they perceive themselves as threatened by an anticipated loss of freedom, a re-do of some previous experience. If things are sufficiently good between you that the altar becomes an option, it's possible that will seriously tilt your sweet and sour ratio. That easily clears the way for an act of thoughtlessness or an acorn argument to grow into the mighty oak of sabotage.

So you need to learn to handle all this gracefully. If one of you makes an exit, and the separation becomes too painful to endure, sit down and ask yourself who saw the altar. If you think sabotage won't appear when the altar pops into view, your relationship is more unusual than most. And when sabotage appears, don't count on figuring out which one of you is responsible; sabotage can be very subtle, and you might have great difficulty identifying its source.

Regardless of its origin, identifying what's happening *as* sabotage is 90 percent of the battle. When you suspect this subtle dynamic is afoot, you and your love need help to explore your suspicions. An hour of professional insight might save the day. Once you identify the cause of the fear and dissention between you, you'll be filled with compassion for your mutual situation. You'll feel compassion because, underneath whatever you think is going on, there is some heartbreaking stuff that's so old and deep it makes the pain of sabotage look like nothing at all. Again, this is an excellent time to invest in the happiness of your relationship. Spend a little time with your coach digging up the poison; it is always less toxic than it seems.

DISTRUST AND CHARACTER

Among the many things that can destroy the green, distrust is surely at the top of the list. If either partner subverts the other's trust, the green fades—perhaps never to be vibrant again. We go on for a while, denying that our relationship has begun to make us sick. The relationship continues to decline, and we become what I call sexual maintenance partners or married singles until someone new comes along.

Bankers, who inevitably deal with issues of trust and distrust all day, have developed a "Five C's" checklist to determine if a borrower is trustworthy. Their client must have Collateral, Cash flow, Capital, Capacity, and Character. The last word on that checklist is frequently used, little understood, and absolutely essential to trustworthiness. Poor character is regarded as synonymous with being untrustworthy and unfortunate.

For our purposes I've defined character as composed of more than just ethical traits. Character is an innate, uncontrived ability to make good things happen—the ability and willingness to create. Because of what we call character, people repetitively reap circumstances that we consider fortunate or unfortunate. A good relationship brings you good fortune; it makes your life easier and more rewarding. Her good character will bring you wonderful breaks just as surely as her poor character will pull you down to her level. For instance, we all know people who rise to highly visible positions and who seem to be honest, yet are later found to be lacking integrity. Their character defect has an obvious adverse affect on their lives and the lives of their family and close associates.

Character is destiny. Character is one of the aspects of human nature that doesn't change very much over a lifetime. So unless you want to be a rescuer, you should probably consider it as permanent as the color of her eyes. Character, trustworthiness, and ethics go hand-in-hand. Lock that concept in your mind—especially as you read chapter 9, "Psychological Landmines."

EROS

The concept of the green incorporates the idea of a whole being greater than the sum of its parts. So when you feel the presence of a warm, wonderful, safe green, your partner is probably enveloped in the same feelings. What's happening for the whole is happening for its parts.

At the onset of a new relationship, the feeling of hot, bright, painfully wonderful, lusty love expands two separate "I's" into a mysterious something called "we." The Greeks named this love after their god Eros. We know him as Cupid who pierces our heart with the arrow of lusty love. If the relationship endures, the Eros stage shuffles everything inside us for about two years before we pass beyond its spell. It's a beautiful gift while it lasts.

But the next stage, Agape (pronounced "ah-gah-pay"), is an even greater gift. Agape brings us subtle love, love that is as sweet as Eros was hot. It's common to mistake Eros for true love, but it's really "true lust." Because we often confuse the two, it's easy to become addicted to Eros and then reject its more beautiful, mature successor Agape. As the ardor of Eros mellows into Agape, the Eros addict fears that love has been lost and sets out to find it again—with someone new.

Eros is so hot, such a siren, that it can only be experienced with a new partner. So, if you set out to find Eros once more, you will have to do it at the cost of losing your present partner, with whom the subtle love, the kind that brings true contentment to the heart, is just being born. Enjoy the Eros-time between you, but look forward even more to Agape, because there you will radiate your true love—your real self—to her. In the silence left by the departing Eros, the self-portraits have dissolved. You begin to connect with one another's souls, deep in your hearts where your spirits merge and where life teaches you to treasure every moment.

WHO MIGHT WE BECOME TOGETHER?

If and when you both find that you're able to work things out, the question you'll ask yourselves is: Who might we become together? If you each love who you are with one another, you can take an important early step toward building a future. What you contribute, not just to each other but to the relationship—to the green—eventually makes heaven or hell on earth. If you're not having a good time, neither of you is entirely to blame; the problem is with the blue *and* the yellow. From your own side of the equation, you need to ask, "What can I do as a 'blue' to make her 'yellow' feel more safe, stable, and open—to allow her to surrender her love into the green where my heart has taken up residence?" The rest is up to her. Watch to see whether she joins you in nourishing the green, in bringing it closer to perfection.

Somewhere along the way, if your "mutual" response doesn't become automatic, the relationship is doomed. Maybe one of you stays permanently needy with the other, or one of you simply doesn't have the capacity to get yourself out of the way and take care of the green. So be it. In that case, *you* don't have the years to waste. Bless the lesson and go elsewhere for the goal—a green that can satisfy and fulfill you.

In the twenty-first century one essential way to find out what kind of green you and your new lady can have is to initiate what I call a "responsible conversation . . ."

"Since we're both being honest, I should tell you I have fleas."

Don't stick it through a knothole
if you don't know what's on the other side.
—Theodore Wentworth

8

KEEPING COMPANY IN THE 21ST CENTURY
RESPONSIBLE CONVERSATIONS

Almost nothing can kill a mood faster than saying the wrong thing at what you thought was the right moment. So it's no mystery that none of us *wants* to discuss sexually transmitted diseases (STDs) with a woman—especially when the relationship is just getting underway and the likelihood of a great evening together is looking bright. But in the contemporary world of dating, giving attention to an ancient Chinese saying can save you a lot of discomfort and embarrassment, and maybe even your life: "Ask a question, and be a fool for a minute. Don't ask and be a fool for a lifetime." As indelicate and unromantic as discussing STDs seems, it is now considered a genuinely caring and respectful thing to do—a way of showing a prospective partner that you think as much of her as you do of yourself. In other words, gentlemen, the game has changed.

Most of us grew up in a world where sexually transmitted diseases were what happened to other people. Now they're what's happening to tens of millions of really nice people just like you and me. Many of those people took most of the right precautions most of the time; many more took some of the right precautions some of the time; and even more thought themselves exempt from danger or didn't think at all and took none of the precautions any of the time. They were in love (in lust) and somehow felt that everything would just magically work itself out once again, and they would be safe.

We can't be cavalier about STDs when 15 million new cases are reported every year in the United States. The good news is that most of these diseases are curable; the bad news is that people often aren't diagnosed—either because they don't have any symptoms or because they don't recognize certain symptoms as related to an STD—so the diseases are easily passed along from partner to partner.

There you are: old enough, savvy, sufficiently wise in the ways of the world, and able to appreciate the power of hormones to override reason. Yet you could have a Ph.D. in STDs and still end up in bed with a nutty choice of partners because someone was lookin' good, baby, the moon was right, and the wine was wonderful. So good that you decided, "The hell with it, we may never meet again"—and thirty minutes later the thought of not meeting again had a certain appeal. (We all know this moment.) Each of you was luring, enticing, and seducing the other with everything in your tool kit. At that level of overwhelm, you cannot expect yourself to deal rationally with the issue of protection against an STD, unless you've decided well ahead of time that *always* using a condom is your policy—period. Then, on the strength of that earlier decision, you're much more likely to take a quick "time out," put on your disease-and-pregnancy protection, and gain the immediate respect of your ready-to-go partner.

We are dealing with a very powerful, primal, sacred energy here. We can still have great fun with it, but its nature requires that we regard this energy with respect—not only for its wonder, but also for the damage it can do. Any two people can go to bed with each other, but they can't leave that bed without consequences. We—you and I—want to keep the consequences in the "wonderful" column. That's not so easy when STDs by themselves carry such a sobering aftermath. You know it, but you don't want to know it: If you don't use protection, *you are, in effect, having sex with everyone your companion has ever slept with.* The same is true for her with regard to you.

It is not my intention to give you a lesson in medical statistics, nor do I want to rain on your dating parade. But I do want you to be thinking with the brain above your waist so you don't play Russian roulette with your health or anyone else's. I do want you to become suspicious of your potential for laxity as soon as you hear yourself say, "Well, she doesn't *look* like she'd have an STD." *You* probably don't look like you'd have one either. Ask yourself, "Is this the hill you want to die on?" And so it is that we come around to the subject of this chapter: responsible conversations in the twenty-first century.

FAMILIARIZING YOURSELF WITH STDs

There are more than twenty-five sexually transmitted diseases, seven of which are considered common. Staying clean sexually requires great care on your part. "I'm sorry" rings hollow if you've passed along an STD to your new life-partner because, a year ago, you were unwittingly contaminated while indulging in an irresponsible exploit. If you think you have an STD, or if you are even slightly suspicious, go to a medical doctor without delay.

The most frequently encountered STDs can be divided into two classifications:

Bacterial
• Chlamydia
• Trichomoniasis
• Gonorrhea
• Syphilis

Viral
• Hepatitis B
• Hepatitis C
• Herpes
• Genital warts
• HIV/AIDS

If you have questions or want more information, please turn to Appendix A, page 173. You might also consult your doctor, check the

Internet, or call the Centers for Disease Control and Prevention National STD Hotline at 1-800-227-8922.

HAVING THE CONVERSATION

A *Los Angeles Times* study estimates that, as of 1997, 45 million Americans have the herpes virus. And did you know that, in world terms, as of 2000, one of every 100 people of reproductive age carries HIV? Faced with such formidable numbers, we can't afford to play the odds until we know one another a lot better. Once you've been together a while and you've become friends, you will have a clearer perspective on those odds.

So, as your relationship becomes sexual, don't be in a hurry until you've gotten the STD discussion out of the way. Do that before you put the condom on the bed table because once you've reached the point of no return, you're not likely to do much talking until afterward. If you find discussing specific STDs too difficult, then at least broach the subject in general terms. Remember, she's expecting the discussion. She will regard it as a genuinely caring and considerate thing to do and will appreciate that you've taken the lead in that way. If you missed the opportunity the first time, do not give up—at least get the discussion behind you before allowing the intense sexual feelings to start again. The discussion of specific STDs is essential. *Don't* wait for her to start it!

Whether or not you think of yourself as being at risk, get an HIV test before you start dating. You can then honestly tell your partner the test was negative. And during the discussion, ask her when she was last tested. That's a perfect lead-in to asking if she's aware of having any other conditions or problems along these lines. Approach the subject with basic kindness and good humor.

Again: *None of this is easy!* Probably all of us would rather avoid such a discussion, because it feels decidedly cool, clinical, and really unromantic. Yet nothing is less romantic or sexy (or more shameful) than you or your partner discovering that the other has an STD and has carelessly passed it on. How do you—or how does she—explain that?

Condoms are a must, at least early in a relationship. Consider it your responsibility to protect yourself and your future—and hers, too. It's not right—and she won't appreciate it—if you ask if *she* brought protection. Once your relationship has progressed to the point where you share strong sexual feelings for each other, you share at least the unspoken (and probably, since you've discussed STDs, a verbal) agreement that you will shortly end up in bed together. Before the clothes come off, just take the condom out of your wallet and place it on the bed table. Your intentions are no secret by then, and if she's the woman you hope she is, she is already considering the problem. *The best way to hold on to the mood of high sexuality is to put the question of protection behind you and have a condom openly within reach when the time comes.*

And while I have your attention with regard to sex and sexuality, let me have a responsible conversation with you about. . .

FRIENDSHIP WITH WOMEN

I have many female friends and want to keep them. I would not choose a mate who was jealous by nature and who would, therefore, strive to curtail my friendships with other women. I am perfectly clear that genuine friendship with a woman who isn't my partner does not allow for any sexual contact. Not that it's against the law—it just doesn't work. I'm absolutely trustworthy and would never subordinate my commitment of faithfulness to my partner while in the company of another woman—even if deep feelings for her should spring up unexpectedly. We can't stop the thought from coming up, but we can stop it from progressing. Never act on it—immediately change the thought, and go on.

EFFECT OF SEXUAL RELATIONS

Sex *immediately* and dramatically changes the nature and dynamics of any relationship. (Yes, I'm sure.) That means sex also changes the nature and dynamics of the relationship with any woman you're dating. (Yes! I'm sure.) Remember the rule: "Anyone can go to bed with someone, but no one gets out of that bed the same."

Do *not* be naïve as to how men differ from women regarding the significance of sex in a relationship, no matter how "apparently" casual that relationship may be. Most women are "hard-wired" to equate sex with love and commitment as opposed to regarding it as just "sport sex." Therefore, if you have sex with a woman, she will most likely take that to mean that your relationship is getting more serious, while you may be thinking nothing of the kind. You may like her well enough, be very turned on, be curious, interested, or whatever, but love is nowhere in your mind! Most women cannot imagine you'd think like that! All I can do is urge you to be sensitive to the fact there are consequences in this area beyond what you think you know.

INFIDELITY

Infidelity doesn't work. That means it doesn't work for *anyone.* You can't have a "good" affair. It doesn't matter whether you're the one in the committed relationship and the Other Woman is unattached, or you're unattached and she is in a committed relationship. Any affair is bad news because it's going to destroy something important. Remember Eros (page 91)? What seems like "just a casual affair" is still going to destroy the intimate, deep, heartfelt agape connection somewhere—certainly between you and your mate, if you have one. No matter which way you turn, it's an emotional tragedy. Nobody wins. Nobody.

"I don't care if she is a tape dispenser. I love her."

S. GROSS

He who chooses the beginning of a road chooses the place it leads to.
—Harry Emerson Fosdick

PSYCHOLOGICAL LAND MINES

A FIELD GUIDE

In the excitement, in the ecstasy of a new connection, your passion might catapult you away from your own best instincts. The purpose of this chapter is to alert you to some of the personality types you may want to avoid but might otherwise not recognize.

While working your plan, you'll want to be alert to significant distortions in a woman's character. If you discover any, you can then decide whether you want to move on or adjust your own conduct and expectations to deal with her behavior. You're about to invest important time and emotions in a relationship with someone. You need to know "when to hold and when to fold."

Consider this chapter a layman's "pathology primer" to help you avoid unwholesome personalities and the inevitable major relationship problems they carry with them. You will want to recognize these personalities and be on your way *before* the relationship becomes long-term. If, after reading this chapter, you still think a relationship with a difficult woman is a good fit for you, it's not too late to discuss it with your coach (see chapter 11) and make plans for how you're going to work with the issues that are certain to arise.

It's important to know that pathology and idiosyncrasy are two different things. Pathology is defined as a serious deviation from a healthy, normal, or efficient condition; it generates serious hardship in people's lives and relationships. Examples include violent behavior; out-of-control spending; addiction to drugs, alcohol, sex, gambling—harmful stuff. An idiosyncrasy is a characteristic, habit, or mannerism peculiar to an individual—for example, cute stuff such as buttering your toast on both sides or singing opera in the shower.

Some idiosyncrasies are merely personality quirks (wearing her sunglasses indoors), while others are troublesome coping mechanisms (ritually checking the stove six times whenever she leaves the house). In this stressful world, we're unlikely to find anyone free of idiosyncrasies—all of us have them—but we *can* expect to be essentially free of pathological characteristics. Relationships are so uniquely personal that you can find happiness together even though you share varying types and degrees of quirks and kinks. However, happiness can be increasingly elusive in the presence of pathology.

While pathology is likely to turn your "green" an ugly color, idiosyncrasies may well make your green better and sweeter than ever. I think people's idiosyncrasies are colorful, and I love to be around colorful people. The challenge is to recognize the difference between "colorful" and "disturbed," since the first can bring you a dynamic happiness, and the other can lead the two of you into a head-on collision.

This chapter won't make you a pro, but it will help you learn to spot problems. That's important, because being fooled—or fooling yourself—is easy. Often you can't see the pathology lying just beneath the surface of certain character and behavior patterns. It's very disheartening to be well into the mission and learn that you've made a big investment in a relationship that's disintegrating.

Before I go into the details of the three major dysfunctional personality types, I want to suggest various *general* ways for you to recognize

104

significant personality problems. I'll discuss some signposts that will help you spot pathology as you travel the path in search of your true love. While you surely won't find serious problems in most women you encounter, you will find it in some—and when you do, the signs will usually be recognizable.

When something just feels "off" about her, and it might be serious, discuss it with your coach and one or two trusted friends. Whether or not you give your therapist a vote in this, he or she is a resource with specialized information and can add an educated, experienced viewpoint to your own. So invite your lady to one or two of your individual counseling sessions. Later on when you're alone with your coach, you will have some fertile soil to plow. You will feel great, knowing you have an established support system ready to help in the crunches. Consider the experience of learning to deal with someone else's stuff part of your adventure.

SIGNPOSTS

Here is a field guide to help you spot psychological land mines you may want to avoid. We're not talking about the normal ups and downs of getting to know each other; we're talking about disturbing characteristics and/or cyclical patterns of behavior that should put you on "red alert" with someone. Everyone is entitled to be "off" occasionally. When that's the case, simply be still—love, encourage, and support her until she comes back on.

But if you realize her wild episodes or bad days are the norm in her life—*and you're being drawn into sharing them with her*—that may be the time for you to cut your losses and say goodbye. If you're vigilant you'll soon be able to recognize whether she's just cycling through something difficult or she's a psychological land mine.

Page one in your field guide should contain the famous and valuable Serenity Prayer from Alcoholics Anonymous:

> *God grant me the serenity*
> *to accept the things I cannot change,*
> *the courage to change the things I can,*
> *and the wisdom to know the difference.*

There are things you *cannot* change—particularly things that are inside another person—and you need the serenity to accept the reality of that. But there are things you can change—inside *yourself*—and you may need to summon the courage to do that. Most of all, it's vital to cultivate the *wisdom* to know the difference—to recognize when serenity is essential and to know when courage is called for.

So, when you become aware that she is experiencing mood swings big enough to pollute the "green," check the following signposts.

Unfinished business. Does she have a lot of unfinished business with others? Consider how long she's been widowed or divorced. Has she had time to go through the process of healing? The actual *amount* of time is not too important; what's more important is her current perspective on the whole experience.

If her previous partner engaged in shockingly hurtful conduct, such as physical or emotional abuse, cheating on her, being financially irresponsible, leaving her in the lurch, committing suicide, or whatever, it is important to notice if that unresolved hurt (that unfinished business) affects her time with you now. A rule of thumb applies: If there's unfinished business you will probably be expected to pay for whatever wounded her in prior relationship(s). Until time and trust in you have healed her lingering fear of additional pain, she'll tend to accuse you or suspect you of similar conduct.

Do you sense that you are somehow responsible for making up for what ol' What's-His-Name did? Is she so jealous that you are expected to prove your fidelity and trustworthiness over and over again? Do you need to wall off most or all of your female friendships regardless of how innocent or long-standing those relationships are? Will you need to prove your love by offering your checkbook as collateral? Is she going to overspend now to make up for financial deprivation in the past? And what about your freedom to be with your children, play golf, or work late without being made to feel like you're abandoning her?

If more than a couple of dates with her are ruined because she's had a disturbing memory, conversation, or encounter related to your predecessor—step back a pace or two and listen carefully. She may be the lesson, not the goal.

Incapacity for successful relationships. Does she speak reasonably well of her late or former husband or boyfriends? Does she have a satisfactory relationship with her children, or are they an endless source of anguish and pain for her? How does she speak of her aging parents? The way she treats her parents and her children might be the way she will treat you after she drops her "self-portrait." It's up to you to decide what constitutes "reasonably well" and "satisfactory" in your situation, but if you notice a negative, critical theme running through her present relationships or through her reports of previous relationships, why would you think her relationship with you will wind up any better? (If pathology is present, you may notice that she has few or no friends or that her friends and family are disturbed or ill-at-ease when they are with her or when they talk about her.)

If she doesn't have the personal capacity to create and maintain warm relationships, you don't need to be another person in her life who "failed" her in some way.

Closed-mindedness. Has she spent any time in therapy and/or doing self-awareness work to increase her understanding of herself, her life, and her relationships with others? Does she scoff at such an idea? Would her life have been wonderful if only so-and-so hadn't done such-and-such? Does she believe something is always wrong with the other people in her life, but she's just fine the way she is? Is she open to the idea that people can learn and grow until the very last days of their lives? If not, prepare to have serious difficulties negotiating what most people would consider normal adjustments between two partners. Don't fool yourself into hoping that a closed mind will magically open someday.

Shared pathology. Through therapy and other self-awareness methods, we have all become much more open about our personal problems, including childhood sexual abuse and other forms of dysfunction in our early environment. The good news is that these subjects don't have to be anyone's skeleton in the closet anymore. The bad news is that, because speaking of such important matters is no longer shameful, people sometimes speak of them too soon in a relationship.

For example, during a low-key lunch soon after you've met, your date hauls out a piece of her agony. You respond compassionately by hauling out a piece of your own, and she feels that she has created instant intimacy. Is this a budding relationship, or is she looking for a therapist, daddy, big brother, or simply another in a long line of male associates who routinely console her about her wretched past? Past pain can turn into shared pathology. That then becomes the main connection between you instead of your sharing beautiful, positive values and matters of mutual interest associated with the here-and-now.

As with so many aspects of a relationship, this is not a "don't ever" matter, as in "don't ever speak of the past." It's a matter of practicing good judgment and appreciating the need to know. Thus, be attentive to her needs and to her tales of past emotional woe, but be cautious if she discusses them too eagerly, too early, or too often in your relationship. Ask yourself how you feel about a woman with a *lot* of problems. Can she let her problems go, or are they replayed over and over? Is there more drama, more unresolved material, than you want to take on at this time in your life? Being with someone should be relatively easy, relaxed, and fun, so the two of you can develop a positive foundation for the bumpier times that life inevitably brings.

Stability versus instability. Is she stable enough for a relationship? I'm going to assume that if you see any signs of alcohol or drug (prescription or "recreational") addiction, food addiction, or unreasonable anger, or if she is a drama queen ("Omygod! The plumber was supposed to be here at ten and he didn't get here till noon—it was a nightmare!"), you will *not* presume that you can "help" or "change" her. Similarly, if she is always changing jobs, owing rent, having a crisis, I'm going to assume that you will wish her well and head on out the door. Why would you volunteer for this?

LAND MINE #1
THE BORDERLINE PERSONALITY:
Tread Lightly Here

"Borderlines" are magnets for drama and will easily fill up the empty spaces in your life. This may have a certain appeal in the midst of your impatience to end the loneliness that has accompanied your loss. The borderline type will have many things you can *do* (to prove your love, be attentive, change yourself, meet her expectations, fill *her* empty spaces, and so on). Since men *like* to be able to do something, to fix things, to find solutions to problems, you'll think she's a perfect match. The problem that arises, however, is that no matter what you do, it's never enough—it might seem like enough for a while, but then your "solution" quickly wears off, and you're back to where you started with her.

The borderline lives out a behavior pattern that's difficult to spot without your investing a considerable amount of time and energy into the relationship. And once you're in deep enough to spot it, escape is difficult because you're already entangled.

Familiarizing yourself with the characteristics of the borderline personality will allow you not only to spot the pattern, but also to decide, before you're in too deep, if you want to be with someone who has it. (Men may have this disorder, too, but it's more difficult to recognize because men are less open with their feelings.)

Bear in mind that mental/emotional "illness" can be broadly defined as *a habitual pattern of normal thought or behavior, exaggerated to an extreme, by someone who ignores all appeals to reason.* Therefore, each of us might exhibit some of the borderline's characteristics under various circumstances. You are watching for definite *patterns* of behavior—relatively habitual ways of functioning. But remember that all of us, including you, have "stuff"; we just need to find someone whose stuff is compatible with our own. So you can date or marry someone with a borderline personality and still be happy. But her borderline characteristics should match your stuff enough for you to be comfortable. For instance, a narcissist can marry a borderline, and they can be a successful couple.

How can you tell whether her conduct is a random event or part of a pattern? You might carve Ian Fleming's words onto some handy place in your brain: "ONCE IS CHANCE. TWICE IS COINCIDENCE. THREE TIMES IS ENEMY ACTION." If she exhibits five or more of the following characteristics, put yourself on alert. If you find all ten, seriously reconsider the relationship. Very seriously.

In listing these characteristics I will refer to "she" and "her," but again, a man can be a borderline as well. A person—man or woman—may have several or all of these traits, and obviously some of the traits have graver consequences than others.

Characteristics of the Borderline Personality.*

1. She is endearing in her own way, so you will be attracted into her "drama." Her behavior tricks you into interpreting it as passion until you realize that you've begun to feel as chaotic inside as she does.

2. She greatly fears being abandoned and will exert frantic efforts to avoid it—whether the abandonment is real or imagined. Partners get stuck trying to prove that they didn't—or won't ever—reject her. They will *never* be able to prove this. Abandonment is a big issue for the borderline.

3. She has a pattern of unstable and intense interpersonal relationships in which she alternates between extremes of idealizing and then devaluing her partner(s). Similarly, she will idealize you one moment and trash you the next, love you this morning and attack you tonight. She is the kind of person who will say, "I've found the *greatest* lawyer [doctor, husband, friend] in the world," and a few days or weeks later be horribly disappointed in or by (and perhaps quite angry at) that same person.

4. She transmits a sense of "attend to me, attend to me." This calls out to your natural rescuer and instills in you a sense of value, a feeling of being needed and important. You then experience a great concern for her (for example, you wake up thinking about *her* life), a desire to take care of her in order to get her out of her current situation and/or misery. You are *her* new best friend. At first it's exciting because you feel competent, useful, and valuable, but eventually you feel your energy being sucked away. You feel exhausted when you're around her or after she's left.

5. She lacks a sense of *your* boundaries—of what's appropriate where you are concerned—and has no boundaries of her own. ("Can I borrow some money?" "Give me your private number at work?" "You can trust me with your car." "I'll do anything for you.") She will be upset when you set limits in this regard.

*This list is adapted from the DSM-IV (The American Psychiatric Association's *Diagnostic and Statistical Manual, Fourth Edition*), from my own personal and professional experience, and from consultation with other professionals.

6. She alternates between extremes of dependency, self-sufficiency, and assertiveness. She constantly manipulates others without their knowing it, turning smiles and tears on and off expertly, or making recurrent threats which either take the form of hints or can be quite direct ("If you don't ____, I will ____"). In extreme cases this can escalate into dramatic but unsuccessful suicide attempts or self-mutilating behavior.

7. Her mood shifts quickly from neutral into depression, irritability, hysteria, or anxiety, usually lasting a few hours and only rarely more than a few days. Her emotions change even more easily than those of someone with a bipolar (manic/depressive) disorder.

8. She demonstrates impulsive, reckless, potentially self-damaging behavior in many areas, such as spending, shopping sprees, shoplifting, casual sex (she often uses sex to prove her desirability), binge eating, vomiting, substance abuse, self-mutilation, reckless driving.

9. Frequent displays of temper, ongoing anger, and even recurrent physical fights are part of how she deals with the world.

10. She exhibits a marked and persistent disturbance in her sense of herself. She will manifest uncertainty about at least two of the following: self-image, long-term goals or career choice, types of friends she desires, preferred values, or sexual orientation. (In other words, you may find yourself wondering what she really wants to be when she grows up.) Under extreme stress, this identity disturbance can become delusional.

The borderline's pattern of behavior may go in cycles—now you see it, now you don't. But ultimately *you will always be busy with her*, always have something to attend to—until you're drained. Then you'll realize what you've gotten yourself into. If you find and value the good qualities in this person enough to want to stay with her, the best way to deal with her is to know what your own limits or boundaries are *and stick to them*—borderlines tend (eventually) to respect definite, consistent limits.

TWO MORE LAND MINES

At the risk of discouraging you from dating altogether, be on the look-out for two more personality types, one of which is an extreme form of the other. The *narcissistic personality* can show up in varying degrees of severity—some you can live with, and others you won't want to. However, if you find yourself in the presence of a sociopath, *run*—don't walk—in the opposite direction.

When you and I were younger, both these personality types existed in the population, but in fewer numbers. We had no need to recognize them or understand how to handle them, because their behavior only rarely touched the lives of "regular" folks.

Now the world has changed—is changing—rapidly and dramatically, and in the midst of those changes we have more people, more cultures, and more complexity to deal with in our human relationships. Consequently, the good news is that you are likely to come in contact with a much wider range of interesting women now than you could have twenty or thirty years ago. The difficult news is that you're subjected to a broader range of psychological problems. Most of the time they're not insurmountable problems, but, as is the case with the borderline, there are two additional "profiles" to protect yourself against.

LAND MINE #2
THE NARCISSISTIC PERSONALITY:
Tread Intelligently Here

Good, strong egos are necessary if we want to be effective. We all need a certain level of narcissism to function socially. Unhealthy narcissists don't have good strong egos—they may look good, but behind the façade they are utterly *self-absorbed*. The common misconception about them is that they are always beautiful, have an exaggerated love for themselves and don't really need other people. They're not always beautiful people and beneath the grandiosity and displays of self-importance, *a big chunk of their identity is missing*—there is an absence of genuine feelings and self-esteem. In a reverse of the borderline profile, we are likely to find more narcissistic men than women, but that ratio is now shifting. As with the borderline, we can look at the characteristics of the narcissist and see some bits and pieces of ourselves; that quality makes them appear "normal." Again, remember that we are looking for a habitual way of functioning and the presence of several character traits that are exaggerated beyond normal so as to become a *troublesome* behavior pattern.

In the narcissistic personality you would see most of the following features:

1. As you spend more and more time with this person, you will notice there seems to be a kind of wall around her. She may be cordial and charming, but there is something impenetrable about her. In situations where you might expect her to show even a small amount of empathy or concern, she doesn't. Indeed, at various times it may seem as if she either doesn't recognize that someone is in distress, or she's almost purposefully withholding any expression of concern.

2. She may exhibit extreme capability, she may be very accomplished in certain areas of her life, but that contains an unspoken message that "I don't need you—or anybody else—for anything." This *looks* self-sufficient, but is actually a total denial of any need on her part for affection, sympathy, or genuine connection. Any suggestion that she might have such needs makes her feel very uncomfortable and can even stir feelings of intense anger and/or depression.

3. She's rather literal-minded and therefore may have a strangely brittle and/or selective sense of humor. Her inability to genuinely laugh at herself coincides with her inability to tolerate criticism, no matter how well-intended. She needs to be attended to and admired constantly, so she experiences criticism as a personal threat, an attack. This is where you'll see that self-sufficient, "can do" shell crumble. She can then turn very cool or very angry as a way of covering her deep sense of humiliation, shame, defeat, or emptiness.

4. Rather than being deep, she is flashy or grandiose and does *not* like to have her behavior interpreted—*she* is different, exempt from categories into which other people normally fall. She is enti-

tled to special consideration or special favors without having to reciprocate; she "shouldn't have to" do what other people would logically do to merit such favors.

5. Similar to the borderline's pattern, the narcissist may alternate between extremes of over-idealization and devaluation in relationships. She thinks of and describes her world in grandiose, inflated terms—"unlimited" success, "total" brilliance, "perfect" love, "unblemished" beauty. She sees suffering as having no value whatsoever.

6. She is also capable of using, exploiting others for her own purposes and can be surprised and angry when people won't do what she wants. Certainty is very important; chance is to be avoided.

7. She has a strange inability to learn from history. She can repeat the same difficult experience on many occasions and treat each occasion as if it were the first time this has ever happened to her. She may have no memory of having told the same story over and over again to the same person. She can remember events that hurt her, but will lie to herself and others about those events in order to present a certain picture of herself (distorting both her self-portrait and her résumé).

LAND MINE #3
THE SOCIOPATHIC PERSONALITY:
Don't Tread Here At All

Lock this in your mind about sociopaths: They operate *very* differently from you and me. You cannot deal with them in terms of how *you* would behave or think in a given situation, and so it's easy for them to come up on your blind side. They are gifted. They are much more clever, controlled, deceptive, and divisive than either the borderline or the narcissist, and when you finally figure out that you have a sociopath in your life, you will be amazed at how completely you were sucker-punched. You might enjoy life with a slight-to-moderate narcissist or borderline, but sociopaths are long-term poison. This is another category more populated by men than by women, but female sociopaths do exist, and it is vital that you be alert to recognizing them early on. If three-quarters of the following traits are present, you have found big trouble.

1. When you encounter them as individuals, sociopaths will seem "larger than life"—too good to be true. And they are. They "hook" into you, they *seem* to connect with you in a way that feels safe and fulfilling to you.

2. They have a superficial—often slick—charm and are able to flatter you with a casual grace.

3. They most often display considerable—in certain cases, even exceptional—intelligence.

4. They are gregarious, articulate, and very convincing regarding what they want you to believe, and they show no apparent signs of delusional or irrational thinking. Their mood swings are shallow, so they *appear* stable and reliable.

5. Disregard for the truth is simply part of who they are, and they camouflage this with a practiced, polished sincerity. They do not appear nervous or neurotic in any context, so they can look straight at you and lie without blinking an eye.

6. Sociopaths *never* feel shame or remorse. They literally have no conscience.

7. They are extremely narcissistic and do not subscribe to values the rest of us deem "normal."

8. They are highly intuitive opportunists—clever, gifted con artists. They lack genuine insight into others, but they are well aware of "working" you—which convinces them that they are superior to you. They get a kind of adrenaline "high" from persuading you to do—or not do—something.

9. They also lack the capacity to display *genuine* emotions or feelings. There is no real depth to their relationships; they are incapable of love, so they use people. They don't have friends who've been there for "the long haul," because they don't have or do *anything* requiring a long haul. Their sexual encounters are just an "act"—part of the con. They're having sex but faking intimacy.

10. They have poor judgment and do not learn by experience; they "score" but never achieve. Over time you will notice strange gaps and inconsistencies in their reports of their personal history.

11. They typically exhibit excellent taste, but that taste leans toward the grandiose.

12. They have a pathological sense of uniqueness and self-importance; their problems are special, their "mission" is special, their talents and achievements are special. And they have a "secret": They *know* they are superior to everyone and are thus "entitled" to special favors and dispensations, exempt from rules that others have to follow.

13. They fail, ultimately, to follow any life plan while often claiming to have one. (Occasionally, this characteristic is not present.)

14. Nothing is ever their fault. They are "misunderstood." Someone else is always to blame.

WHAT'S NORMAL?

Keep in mind that in any examination or evaluation of personality, there is such a thing as a healthy self-regard, and no such thing as a "completely" normal person. Fortunately, only a very small percentage of our population would be grouped in the cluster we would call "utterly pathological."

But, again, with our burgeoning world population, the rapid technological dissolution of many old boundaries between people, and the enormous changes in the traditional family structure, people are growing up and showing up in a greater variety of interesting variations on the human theme. We are freer to go places, to know, to do and be more than we ever imagined. That freedom provides us with endless possibilities for interesting encounters and fertile ground for a wider variety of disturbed people as well.

These descriptions are not meant to alarm you. Pathologically disturbed women are the exception. But you should know enough so that you can recognize potential problems to discuss with your coach. This strategy will not only lead you to the woman who is just right for you, but will also save you time, energy, money, and heartbreak. Stay sharp, listen up, look carefully, think clearly, and follow your instincts instead of your hormones—and most of the women you meet will be anywhere from just okay to really terrific.

Weeks or months later, as you glide down even the shiniest of yellow brick roads with the woman you *know* is the most terrific person you've ever met, you can expect a few real-world speed bumps. Let's look at what to do and how to think when you hit them.

"The way I see it is, we're both serious, but about different things."

10
FIGHTING
CLEARING THE AIR AND STAYING FRIENDS

At some point, all couples need ways to express their discomfort about certain aspects of their relationship. When you begin to share and discuss your discomfort with each other, the skills you both have available will determine whether you gradually build or gradually destroy the trust and intimacy between you.

Plenty of information is available on how to resolve disputes. This chapter is intended to do no more than whet your appetite for more knowledge and encourage you to search on. What follows is a look at some of the stuff that comes up when couples face their differences and attempt to resolve them by means of suggestions, discussions, arguments, and/or fights.

SUGGESTIONS

Suggestions sound like: "Would you like to . . . ? Or "I'd feel more comfortable if . . . " Or "What would happen if [we bought a new car]? Or "What if we [take a walk together every night after dinner]—I think we'd [both have more energy and feel better if we exercised every day]."

DISCUSSIONS

If she agrees to walking every night and then turns you down five or six times, it's time for a discussion. So how are you going to approach the subject? You might say: "Remember when I suggested that we walk after dinner, and you agreed? I thought you meant that, but apparently you didn't. Can we talk about this?" She might say something like: "Well, I don't like feeling controlled." Following which you might add: "So what you're saying is that you agreed with me just to shut me up. I don't like that." (You could be softer here, but challenging her like this works for our example.) She [hitting back]: "Me either, but I also don't like feeling controlled."

ARGUMENTS

This conversation is going in one of two directions. It's going to escalate into an argument, or one of you—if not both of you together—are going to redirect the discussion away from an argument to the issue at hand. Stick to specific issues. Here, the specific issue is whether the two of you will take walks after dinner. If too many things are thrown on the table at this point, the discussion will become generalized, and you'll find yourselves looking at a mass of issues (such as everything you have ever argued about together) that neither of you can talk about without having hurt feelings. Hurt feelings make you (or her) want to strike back, and then you've got a fight.

To direct your conversation away from an impending argument, you might say: "Let's leave the other issues till later. Right now, let's just talk about walking and what that has to do with control. Let me ask you this: is walking with me a pleasure for you?"

She: "Yes, but I hate walking at night. I'd rather be cozy with you in

120

front of the fire. I'd actually prefer walking before breakfast in the morning."

You: "Great. I needed to know that. When would you like to start?" (If you say: "How about tomorrow morning," you might be controlling again. Leave the start time up to her.)

Then, you might close the discussion with a hug to express your appreciation for resolving the conflict. Now you've not only cleared up the walking issue but engaged in successful problem-solving as well.

FIGHTS

No two people can agree on everything, and voicing differences is important to the life of any relationship. Passionate disagreement is positively human. If there's a good flow of communication, you'll solve the problem and categorize your squabble as one of the common annoyances of being with another person. That kind of conflict—a "good" fight—not only clears the air but restores intimacy.

A "bad" fight—one in which the verbal gloves come off—can permanently damage your relationship if you're not careful. Serious damage occurs when you start bullying each other, when each of you is focused on proving that the other's point of view is trivial, stupid, or wrong, or when you begin making personal attacks. *You're engaged in a personal attack when you make her wrong or diminish her sense of her own worth or capacity so that she believes she is less of a person.* In short, don't demean her—ever. It is the single most damaging tendency in a relationship. You want to shoot the problem, not one another.

If the discussion about walks after dinner had escalated from the specific to the general to the point of her saying, "You try to control everything I do," you probably would have launched yourselves into a full-tilt, unproductive, bad fight. To avoid this, your own best move (and hers, too) is simply to stop and declare a time-out when you see the fight taking shape. That way, both of you can calm down, recover emotionally, and allow things to return to the discussion level, where real progress can happen. Healthy negotiation is the name of the game here. In arguments and fights, people are usually concerned with making themselves right, with *winning at the expense of the other person.* In a discussion—even an intense one—everybody can win.

FIGHT-O-PHOBIA

"We never fight," you say.

Too bad for you. "Fight-o-phobia" can be deadly to a relationship. Human beings cannot be together day after day and go around smiling *all* the time. It's an impossible feat. Someone is not telling the truth, and eventually one of you will start walking toward the door. You need to come up with ways to identify a controversy so you can discuss it before you have to stuff it. People do not—*cannot!*—live together without disagreements. It's the *skill* with which you manage your disagreements that saves the day.

FIRST FIGHTS

When the wonderful—but unrealistic—"bliss bubble" has popped, when real life has presented itself, and you and your lady have your first fight, pay attention! First fights provide very important information that can be a reality check for both of you.

If you pay attention when the fighting starts, you'll probably discover parts of one another you didn't know about. What you observe at this point can be very reassuring—or give you insight that will save you a lot of trouble later. When it's over, either you'll have developed a deeper trust because you've learned that you fight fair together, or you'll have seen the red flag of "irreconcilable differences" waving in your direction.

In many ways a first fight means that you feel comfortable enough with each other to display your unhappiness, concern, or displeasure about something—i.e., "I care enough to fight with you instead of sweeping this under the rug and bashing you with it later." Or: "I respect and love you enough to fight about this, and I trust your sense of yourself is strong enough that you won't get blown away by our difference of opinion."

Disagreements serve to remind us that there are, after all, two individuals in a relationship. If you forget that, there is trouble ahead: You'll be particularly vulnerable once the initial, lusty stage of your relationship has passed, and you may never progress to the magic of the later, even more rewarding stages.

FIGHTING—THE RAW MATERIAL

Fighting can be dissected into two parts:

1. What we're *apparently* fighting about (the reason for this particular fight)
2. What we're *really* fighting about (the deeper pattern of conflict)

Couples fight over specific things like money, the raising of children, schedules, politics and religion, each other's dashed expectations, what one of them is wearing tonight—you name it. The topics, and therefore the apparent reasons, are as varied as the human condition allows.

Couples also argue over less specific things, such as their individual tolerance levels for both distance and closeness. I may need a lot more time alone than you do. You may need a lot more social time than I do. We usually don't know these "rules" about one another until we've been together for a while. We must be alert when evidence of their existence pops up, so we learn to predict, recognize, and negotiate them on the spot instead of fighting about them. If one of you isn't happy, that's a problem for both of you. *Honoring each other's needs* builds your mutual goodwill account and reduces the reasons to argue.

Couples can also be masters at fighting over nothing. You become upset that your partner became upset about something, and she's upset that you became upset that she became upset, etc. This can become hurtful, go on into infinity, and send the two of you to your separate corners. When you look at what the argument was about, you can't find any reason for it other than hurt feelings and guilt over causing pain for the other person. My wife and I have our black belts in this pattern.

What you're *really* fighting about is harder to recognize. That's because it arises from the long-term patterns of behavior between you, the unspoken "contract" you've worked out regarding how difficulties are going to be addressed and dealt with. Therefore it has become part of a nearly invisible background of your relationship.

A classic example: Jack comes home from work, he's really tired and doesn't want to deal with his wife Mary, or the kids—it's all too much. All he wants is a twenty-minute break, but he doesn't know how to say, "I've had it, I need twenty minutes alone to catch my breath." Instead he walks through the door with "that look" on his face. She knows the look. Angry and hurt at her husband's rejection of her and their family, she shuts down and turns away with an exasperated sigh.

This is an emotionally expensive ritual, and it delivers much more than the twenty-minute breather Jack wanted. Now he has an entire evening of separation, distance, and bad feelings—for which he blames her.

You can see this fight is part of a deeper pattern than what appears on the surface. It's an example of acting out feelings instead of asking for what he needs; poor communication skills lead Jack to emotionally abuse his family. Mary's response gave him the space he needed—and regardless of the cost, he will do it again. The relationship is weakened, his wife feels powerless and will now do something in retribution—and the pattern is perpetuated.

WHY DO WE FIGHT

1. **Honest anger.** Genuine anger has a purpose. I may have been disappointed; or I don't like something you've done; or I don't like the way something is going; or I don't like the way I'm feeling about something between us—and I want things to change. And/or I want *you* to change. So, a significant amount of emotional steam rises, and we label that "anger."

2. **Unspoken issues.** Certain issues remain unspoken and certain feelings remain unexpressed because we fear an argument. We fear arguments because we're not accustomed to thinking of them as vehicles for productive change. We see a fight as a sign of trouble, rather than as a signal that something is struggling to find expression between us. That "something" can be as threatening as a pack of ravenous wolves (last week's unresolved blowup about how you seem hostile toward her children) or seem as insignificant as a mosquito (this morning's gentle complaint about failing to come to the table when she calls) but, in any event, it *needs* attention. And if you think a mosquito isn't significant, you've obviously never had one in your bedroom on a hot summer night.

3. Resentments. Resentments arise when there's an unresolved "something" between you that you chose to bury. The effect of large resentments (she cheated on me) on a relationship is obvious. Small resentments (she's always fifteen minutes late) build as they are left undiscussed over time—perhaps due to your good intention not to "make a big deal" out of something. If you've got only one, slowly growing, "three-ounce" resentment, you can easily toss it over your shoulder and be done with it. But after you've tossed a second, third, and fourth one, you have a growing collection that eventually fills a gunnysack. One day you wake up and discover you have a fifty-pound gunnysack full of three-ounce items, and you start hurling it around the room. You can really hurt someone that way. Stay on top of your resentments. Don't let them hide out or pile up in your mind or emotions. Talk about them before they suck the life out of the relationship. In determining whether your relationship is a "keeper," resentments and how they're handled offer important information to you and your partner.

4. Need for time out. As mentioned in a previous example, we sometimes use arguments as a way of taking a breather without realizing what we *really* want. Often, our being straightforward about asking for some "alone time" is surprisingly difficult. Somehow that request can be interpreted to mean, "You don't want to be with *me*." So, we worry about telling our mate what we need. (And we don't feel that great if our mate delivers the same message to us.) As a result, we stifle our real desire and unconsciously start a fight to get the time we need. For example, you're mad at her. That means you don't have to talk to her for the rest of the day or have sex with her tonight. Or you can leave the house for the afternoon.

But then you have a dilemma: What you're fighting about—just to get some personal space—has taken on a life of its own. Now you must fix something that wasn't broken in the first place.

5. Habitual stress. Sometimes we fight because we're stressed. When we're stressed—or over-stressed—or we feel uncomfortable in our own skin, we tend to strike out against those who are nearest and dearest. This is a common but nasty habit to fall into.

6. **Attitude.** When we transmit anger, fear, or frustration through body language, tone of voice, or attitude, we make life hell for the people around us. It's a poor workman who curses his tools, and it's a poor, ignorant man who emotionally abuses his loved ones. We need to take "nice lessons" from a role model to teach us to handle anger, fear, and frustration in ways other than body language, tone of voice, and aggressive conduct.

Bad attitude is a major trigger for disputes. It's what makes people say to you: "You can't talk to me like that," or "Don't use that tone of voice with me," or "You don't have to be nasty—I just asked you a simple question." You're usually not aware of this behavior in yourself, so when someone calls it to your attention, you'll hear yourself saying: "I didn't mean it like that" or "If I ever do it again, just ignore it." Those responses beg the question and give you ongoing permission to be an asshole. You've made it the other person's responsibility to edit your obnoxious delivery, even though it's absolutely *your* problem.

Incidentally, your abuse of someone is not a freebie. Count on most of your victims getting even with you through passive-aggressive behavior. Read on about fighting styles.

DIFFERENT FIGHTING STYLES

Most people's fighting "styles" can be traced to their experience growing up. If you saw positive, productive disagreements between your parents, you probably learned how to fight constructively. If your parents demeaned each other when they fought, or one parent yelled and the other capitulated, then fighting looked like a battle for control. So you either duplicate their style or you avoid arguing because you don't want to control like your "mean" parent, nor do you want to be controlled like the passive one.

If your parents fought constantly without resolving anything, and all that was left was a pile of bad feelings, you may have learned that's simply "what couples do." So you learned to fight dirty; or, because it looked so ugly and pointless, you made an early decision not to fight at all. And finally, if your parents never fought, or fought in private, then you have no model for what works.

Whatever your background, it's safe to assume that you and your partner will have different fighting styles. You'll need to *learn* about hers and vice versa. She may need to blow up and get it over with fast. You may need to go away and organize your thoughts for half an hour before you can talk with her about a problem. Each of you will interpret these *temperamental* characteristics in different ways—probably judging them negatively at first, because they're not like your own.

Regardless of what you think of as your "style," keep in mind that yelling, throwing things (going ballistic), or stomping out of the room brings only temporary satisfaction—and can open a wound that may never heal. Conversely, artificially keeping the peace by repressing your anger leads to anxiety, depression, and loss of self-respect.

Often partners who don't think they're really fighting or who believe they're above it all are engaged in *passive-aggressive* behavior—the "water torture." This is actually covert aggression, a powerful and relentless style of fighting. Don't be fooled: The passive-aggressive person delivers angry retribution but without ever appearing angry. She feigns a headache to deprive you of sex, thus punishing you for making her angry or hurting her feelings. Perhaps she overdraws her bank account or goes on a shopping spree. Passive-aggressive behavior saps your energy and is every bit as damaging as screaming and yelling.

We all want to feel heard! Is she important enough for you to work with her—*after* a fight—to change what you're arguing about? Can you laugh at yourselves? Is one topic on the table more often than another? Is there a rhythm or predictable cycle to your arguments?

You have to be careful about making her hormones responsible, but PMS (premenstrual syndrome) or menopause really *can* be a factor here. If either applies, you'll want to raise the issue carefully when her cycle is in balance. Informing a woman that her hormones are out of whack—*when* they are out of whack—is like stepping in front of a firing squad. Couples are wise to keep track of this with a calendar if they notice some kind of three weeks "on," one week "off" cycle. Be kind when she's vulnerable.

PMS or not, couples may unconsciously establish cycles for fighting as an intimacy regulator to adjust the sweet-and-sour ratio. For example, you seem to get along really well for eight days, and on the ninth you always have a fight. Sometimes things are just too good for too long and you need to stir them up. Baffling but true.

Consider, too, that men and women tend to have different styles

127

regarding anger. Women often wait for cues that help them feel emotionally safe and cherished before they fully express who they are. (Remember the woman who did not initially disclose her desire to walk in the morning instead of at night.) They don't want to put themselves into a position to be rejected. This can mean that a woman will keep quiet for too long about something that troubles her—especially in the initial stages of a relationship. But, unwittingly, she may be collecting injustices to dump on you later in an emotional explosion.

EMOTIONAL ABUSE

What you—or your partner—think of as "anger" may be nothing more than a polite name for emotional abuse. Any conduct that *threatens* to, or actually does *punish, shun, harangue, shame, deprive, or disgrace* the other person(s) is emotionally abusive. Don't expect to wave a magic wand and have the abuse disappear. Get help.

What constitutes emotionally abusive conduct? It's probably present if one of you:

- has a mean streak or a wild temper;

- resorts to violence in the form of threats, physical combat, or breaking cherished possessions;

- goes crazy over something that really isn't a big deal;

- becomes silent and uncommunicative in the face of something that is important and troubling to the other;

- digs his or her heels in on a position—and that's that;

- holds a grudge for an extended time—for instance, dragging an issue out for days or months; or

- punishes the other for arguing—for example, if either of you withholds sex or affection or spends beyond the credit limit even after it seemed you had settled the argument (a classic example of passive-aggressive behavior).

128

PROTECTING YOUR RELATIONSHIP
"BANK ACCOUNT"

Think of a relationship as an account you have with each other. If either of you takes from the relationship more than you contribute—whether by fighting, passive-aggressive behavior, or by other means—you deplete the relationship just as surely as you deplete your bank account by taking out more than you put in.

One of the most effective ways to build your relationship account with a partner is to contribute plenty of good emotions, feelings, gestures, validation, and caring. If you have an argument or disappoint your partner after you've built up plenty of credits, you will have enough goodwill available to help you bridge the problem.

Empathy and thoughtfulness add greatly to your account, too. When you understand that what you're doing is having an impact on what she's doing, you're empathizing with her. Most men benefit from empathy training. By learning this skill, you will recognize how you are responsible for some of her problems, since her actions may be reactions to something you've said or done.

A couple adds to their relationship account whenever they actively seek to meet one another's differing needs and desires. For instance, a man usually has sex as a first priority, while a woman wants affection. A woman thinks in terms of sincerity, and in giving herself she gives her heart. Telling her "You look so lovely"—and meaning it—is more valuable, and probably gets more credits, than giving her jewelry. Complimenting her sincerely fills her with your affection, whereas the jewelry might be nothing more than you proving your credentials—an offering of what you are in the world's eyes, but *not* an offering of yourself or of your affection.

Women in loving relationships don't weigh the gift; they weigh the sincerity and affection behind the gift. They often don't treasure an insincere "trophy" gift as much as a sincere offering that acknowledges something you've noticed about them. Whether you arrive at the door with one rose or five dozen, you win—if the giving conveys your commitment, interest, and a sense of affection. (Incidentally, there's a big difference between your affection for her and how high you can jump. The latter is not about her. It doesn't include her. She merely gets to watch and "marvel" at how accomplished you are.)

When you're thinking of a gift, by the way, select it with *her*—not you—as the focus. Look for ways to make her happy rather than showing her how important you are or what you can do for her. Giving both of you ten sessions in a cooking school might mean more to her than an expensive cruise. This is not about money, it's about "style." Your emotional availability and capacity for intimacy are what will impress her most.

Dazzle her with your *heart*, with how important she is in your life, with how much you love her. If you don't know what I'm talking about, you have some serious work to do. Take a weekend course on relationships or ask your coach for some insight on intimacy and emotional availability. It's an area where women are especially sensitive and most men are sound asleep.

THE "GOOD" FIGHT

Once the two of you have built a substantial relationship account, you've greatly improved your chances for having productive disagreements and settling them quickly. However, there are rules of engagement.

A good fight is a fair fight. Keep the discussion specific to the problem. Whether suggesting, discussing, arguing, or fighting, the basic challenge lies in being able to keep the *problem* in your sights—aiming at *it* and not at each other.

Keep expressions like "You always . . ." or "You never . . ." out of your brain and out of the fight. "When you walked in here, you didn't hug me" can be dealt with in a couple of minutes. "You never hug me" can lead you into an argument that tracks back over years and goes on for five hours.

Listen to her! Work to understand the point of view behind her anger even if you don't agree. If you have words in your mouth ready to speak before your partner is through speaking, you're assuming a defensive posture rather than listening. This is not the time to try to be "right"—it's better (and safer) to listen, without interruption, until she empties.

One way to be sure she's emptied before you interrupt is to invite her to hold an object (a book, a pillow, etc.) in her lap until she's done.

Then she hands it over to you, and you offer your viewpoint. When you're through, hand the object back to her and once again listen intently to what she is saying. This technique makes room for both of you to empty to each other. It also prevents you from pouncing on her lines and disorienting her thoughts. And it calms your need to have a lightning-quick and totally-right response on the tip of your tongue should she take a breath.

A useful technique is for you to summarize back to her what you *believe* she's said, so she knows you're listening to her. For example, you could say: "Let me see if I've got this right. You're upset because I didn't . . ." When you do this, you acknowledge having heard her point, and you clear the way for her to say more of what's on her mind.

Making an appointment to review grievances can be very helpful. At times, problem-solving can be postponed by common consent in order for you to give one another your full attention instead of hurried or exhausted impatience. You can usually be tolerant and pleasant if you know you have set time aside to solve problems. "This isn't a good time for me to discuss this. Can we both explore it at lunch on Thursday?" This is not you trying to put her off, and both of you must follow through with—or renegotiate—the Thursday lunch.

Don't forget the occasional good trade: "I'll go to the ballet if you'll come to the races with me" is a fair give-and-take, even though you hate the ballet and she doesn't like the races.

And remember, one road out of a fight is to offer an apology. Even if you don't want to apologize, you *can* say, "I'm sorry for upsetting you." (You probably did do that much, right?) Such an apology offers a neutral but sincere invitation to move on.

The "good fight" ends with both partners feeling emotionally safe, feeling that no cloud is hanging over their heads. Neither one of you feels resentful, nor is either of you going to retaliate or punish the other by becoming passive-aggressive.

BIG DAMAGE ITEMS

Don't let fights be contaminated by alcohol. Too many fights are started and prolonged this way. Accumulating grievances is bad enough, but when alcohol releases them you're likely to do even more damage than if you stuffed them a while longer. Good fighting, like safe driving, requires good sense and a clear head. Don't drink and fight.

If you make the fight personal, you will leave a scar. *Never* make it personal. If you call someone a "dumb bitch," "whore," "fat cow," or "incompetent," those terms stick and are emotionally abusive. They are curses that will follow you both. They will not only wound her self-esteem, but she will also get even with you through passive-aggressive behavior. Once this stuff comes between you, it hangs all over the house like bats.

Some points to keep in mind:

- Never call one another "stupid." What someone *said* might seem stupid to you, but the other person—personally—is never stupid.

- Never make one another beg.

- Never threaten to end the relationship in order to win the argument or stop discussion.

- Never demean one another. Success comes from empowering others, since, in that way, you subtly (and acceptably) empower yourself.

- Never play the role of a parent scolding a disobedient child or allow her to do that with you.

- Don't invalidate her point or her thinking. Find what's right about what she said and then *add* your own point to it, rather than contradicting hers. For instance, if you're five minutes late and she's angry because you didn't call, don't say, "I'm not late." Say, "I know you'd like me to call if I'm going to be late, but I didn't think that five minutes was 'late.'" And now is the time for you to renegotiate the agreement: "How about if I call when I'm going to be late by thirty minutes or more?" She feels heard, and you get to change something you regard as burdensome.

- Don't say: "So what we're going to do is . . ." Instead, enlist her by asking, "What if we . . . ?" or "What would happen if we . . . ?" or "Can we . . . ?" or "What do you think about . . . ?"

WHEN THE DUST HAS SETTLED

Even if your partner passes all the tests and has all the goodwill in the world, you and she are still different. She has a different history and different interests and different genetics. Henry Higgins pleaded, "Why can't a woman be more like a man?" Thank God she's not! There is a maxim that when you want to know what a woman is thinking, ask her how she feels, and when you want to know what a man is feeling, ask him what he thinks. Women talk about problems to feel better, and men talk about problems to get an answer. Women see the world through wonderfully different eyes than we do. Women understand men far better than men understand women. The desires of men and women differ, *and* the ones we hold in common (for example, sex and affection) tend to get prioritized differently.

That does not make either one of us right or wrong. Just different.

"Maybe you ought to consider making love in the morning—before you have a chance to piss each other off."

He that won't be counseled can't be helped.
—Benjamin Franklin

11

THE THERAPIST AS A RESOURCE

FOR ME OR FOR US

So, why is a shrink so important? *You're* not a nut case!

People of high accomplishment acknowledge the value of having a coach, a mentor, or a guide. We all know that athletes training for the Olympics need a coach. Begin to think of yourself as preparing for your own "Relationship Olympics." Finding the best—the Mrs. Right-For-You—without screwing things up or perhaps even destroying them will take every skill you have and therefore cries out for a coach to give you insight and perspective. That's why a shrink is so important.

In the arena of love you don't want to settle for minimums. This is the rest of your life. You know what wonderful looks like—you might have had a great relationship yourself—yet just living creates a lot of emotional baggage for us all. To start working on a miracle of your own, you will benefit from someone who can do for your new life what an interior designer does for your home or office.

135

Men probably take longer to bond to their partner than women do, but once they form a bond and lose it, their feelings of loss can be profound. If that sounds like you, you may be so hurt that you'll want to find a coach without delay. Someone else might not feel the need for a coach for the first six to eight months. Following your loss, you will probably have a great deal of support from understanding friends and loved ones. You may feel that you don't need more than that, because those around you know how to listen and just what to say. But as everyone's daily life goes on, that support will diminish, and your need for a coach will become more pressing.

So, now or shortly, it's time for a head coach—a psychologist or an MFT (marriage and family therapist). Those licenses are hard to come by, and the people who hold them study for up to eight or ten years, including internship. During their internship they learn the moves from the already accomplished and then take written and oral state licensing exams to prove they know their subject. They're experts who are trained to help you understand, repair, and/or remodel your life from the inside out.

Having a coach is playing to win. It takes insight and practice to gain the skills necessary to have an enduring relationship that's really rich. This doesn't happen by accident. You don't want to look back on a relationship that could have brought you deep, enduring happiness and realize that you destroyed it because you didn't know how to handle the twists and turns.

FINDING A COACH

Finding a therapeutic coach isn't hard. Friends or colleagues might already be involved in counseling, so you can ask them who they are seeing. You can then explore whether you want to see one of those therapists or ask them for a referral instead. As far as I'm concerned, family doctors, lawyers, or twelve-step sponsors are *not* qualified to act as your coach, but are wonderful sources for a referral. As a good last resort, check the yellow pages under psychologists or psychotherapy, or look for a local chapter of a psychological association.

You may need to interview more than one therapist in order to find someone who is not only good, but whom you feel you can relate to. If a therapist won't personally respond to your call, give priority to the therapist(s) who will. The process is similar to dating, in that one of the most essential aspects of the relationship with your new coach is your chemistry together. You will feel more comfortable with the interviewing process once you have made a few calls and have developed a better idea of what you are looking for. Here are some questions for you to consider before and during a conversation:

- Do you prefer to see a man or a woman? (Some men choose a woman, because we already know how men think. We might believe that a female's insight into us—and eventually into our potential partner and then into the relationship—could provide an especially valuable viewpoint.)
- Do you want the therapist to be older or younger? (Close to your age is my preference—no more than seven years either way.)
- Do you feel a connection with this person?
- Do you feel safe?

Will this therapist be your coach or your boss? I think you'll want to grow—not obey. You're looking for someone to assist you with *your* plan rather than your having to work the therapist's plan. But if you feel you might want more direction, find someone you can truly respect to give it to you.

After gathering a few referrals (or leads), call the therapists and tell them you have just been through a death or divorce and you think the advice of a professional could make your experience easier. This phone call is your first opportunity to interview the therapist. Listen to how he or she responds. Are you just hearing "uh-huh" on the other end, or do you have a feeling that this is someone who's interested—who can give you insight and genuinely care about you? You can ask questions such as:

- How long have you been in practice?
- Do you have a specialty?
- Do you work with couples?
- Are you married or have you ever been married? (In your situation, this is a valid personal question.)
- Have you ever lost a spouse to death or divorce?
- What do you charge?
- Do you charge for the first appointment?

There are no right or wrong answers to these seven questions. They are just ways of gathering information so you can decide if you'd be comfortable with the person on the other end of the phone

NO COACH

As you progress through the stages of grief and loss, you'll need a way to release your feelings. Bottling them up inside or dumping them on others will drive listeners away. It won't work for you to continually talk about your loss with those around you. You need to express your feelings, but friends don't know how to respond adequately, beyond a certain point, because they're not trained—and your experience isn't happening to them. Dumping or purging your feelings eventually becomes very awkward for them *and* you. You may alternate between feeling emotionally distant and withdrawn, then suddenly become needy; others may eventually feel sucked dry and will learn to avoid you. That is what you *don't* want. So, here's the deal: *Hire a coach or lose your friends.*

WHAT YOU CAN EXPECT FROM COACHING

1. A coach/therapist/"shrink" can be a lifeline who helps you stay connected by relieving those around you of having to deal with your grief.

2. You may need to repetitively—over and over again—"download" your feelings of grief over your loss; your coach is there to listen to *all of it.*

3. As you progress, a good coach will not let you dwell on your grief indefinitely; rather, at the right time, he or she will gently nudge you along, urging that you move beyond the grief—and that's what you want. Your loved ones don't want to see you in pain, they don't want you to grieve endlessly, and they don't want you dragging your negative feelings around.

4. Being coached through your grief and loss will free you up emotionally. You will move more quickly out of denial and through the stages of anger, bargaining, depression, and acceptance.

5. As you encounter the world of dating, your intentions will shift. You may initially just want a female companion. As you continue, your intent may shift toward a more serious commitment. This is the time to have your coach already in place and familiar with your goals and strategy, so that, like a self-correcting missile, you are always moving toward your target without delay and with few errors.

6. Your coach will help you recognize the consequences of your own behavior and assist you in evaluating whether your plans are on target or you're just fooling yourself.

7. Your coach will help you better understand who you are dating and whether or not you're a good match.

8. There are risks in the world of dating. You want to extend your heart to a potential mate, but you may subconsciously fear re-experiencing the emotional pain of another loss. When a new relationship does not work out, your feelings of loss can piggy-back on the original loss of your spouse, and you feel like you've been thrown back to square one. It's important not to become paralyzed here, but to survive the lessons leading you to your ultimate goal. Your coach can be a big help in identifying your feelings, and their source, and in modulating your responses.

9. You will unload huge emotional baggage, reduce your vices, and learn to recognize repetitive behavioral and emotional patterns that have left you unfulfilled.

10. A coach will encourage you to welcome new experiences.

11. A coach can help you enliven dulled feelings and develop more empathy and compassion for yourself and those around you. You will gain a greater awareness of who you are and learn to forgive yourself. You will see that at any given moment you did the best you could, given your current coping skills. Forgiving yourself leads to forgiving others.

BOTH OF YOU TOGETHER

I urge you to get past the idea that therapy has no value unless your relationship is in trouble. You may eventually decide to include your new partner in your meetings with your coach. Couples counseling will refresh and enlarge your capacity for intimacy and strengthen your ability to communicate—objective insight can be a great help to all relationships. It can certainly help you avoid pitfalls along the way as you and your partner develop your relationship. In other words, it helps clean up your blue and her yellow, so that the green flourishes and charms you both.

On your journey, you can be lucky enough to find the lady with whom you want to begin the next chapter in your life. The ecstatic opening stages of that romance, however, may delude you into believing that you can now just relax and coast—that finding love has solved your problems and hers, too.

But remember coming together with your first wife? In the beginning she seemed like a perfect diamond. All you could see was her beauty and luster until you gradually became aware of her flaws. Then, with time, you learned to look past those flaws and see her real inner beauty. Likewise, your new lover may be a diamond too, and some of her flaws will probably be different from what you've previously experienced. Your coach can help you deal with those flaws as well as your own so that they don't combine to destroy your new relationship.

You and your partner are attracted to each other for a variety of reasons. In addition to the love you share, you're also drawn together (whether you realize it or not) to grow and to support one another in becoming the most that you can be. The ease with which you endure the growing pains as you come together will determine the ease of your relationship.

In fact, on a very subtle level, you and your mate will be negotiating how much intimacy the two of you can handle. You may consciously believe that you want to develop a greater intimacy between you, yet subconsciously you may be rejecting such closeness. Exploring and deepening intimacy ("into-me-see") requires that you share your vulnerabilities, that you expose the softest parts of you to your partner—

the parts you'd rather not expose. This is where you might begin to *sabotage* what could potentially be the next great love of your life. And, once again, this is where you will want your coach.

Real change takes time and effort. Be patient. Coaching is a process, not a product. You're not looking for a quick fix, but for growth that will last a lifetime. Books and other forms of information are good for insight and help steer you in the right direction. *However, insight does not change behavior. Experience does.* Therapeutic coaching allows you to alter your very core; in the process, you can earn the equivalent of a college degree—in yourself. What a gift!

"I'm sorry, Nathan, but I need to color outside the lines."

No act of kindness, no matter how small, is ever wasted.
—Aesop

12

BREAKING UP

GENTLY, CONSIDERATELY

Keep your search on track by *artfully* extricating yourself from a relationship that does not meet your goal. If the relationship has progressed beyond dating, you will want to make your exit as elegant as possible. Using the skills we'll cover in this chapter, you can manage to do that—dissolve a problematic or unfulfilling relationship with the least damage or hurt to either of you.

When you recognize that an inevitable change is coming in your relationship, you'll be better off if you help it happen sooner rather than later. But doing that in the very best way, doing it gracefully, can be a challenge.

When you begin to recognize that things have deteriorated and the time to break off has arrived, assume you are being shown that you have been in a relationship that was a lesson instead of the goal. The dissolution—and disillusionment—parading before you is not about fault or blame. The issue is that there was something for both of you to learn, and now you have simply grown beyond each other. *If* you got the lessons, you go on to fulfill a new piece of your heart's desire. If you *didn't*, you redo the lessons until you get them so well that you won't bring damage to your new love.

It's natural to try to support a faltering relationship, to try to make things better before you ditch it for good. But if it recovers only temporarily and never "grows," it's time to say goodbye. Don't assign blame either to yourself or her. When a relationship is truly fading, you don't have a lot of choices. You can watch it get worse, you can lie to (or avoid) her, or you can leave with grace and kindness.

If you catch yourself bullshitting, listen up! Women use terms like "sleazebag," "slimeball," "scumbucket," "jerkface," or "asshole" to describe men who lie or "avoid" their way out of a relationship. Be open and direct. Do you need more time to yourself? Tell her. Are you afraid to speak about something that's annoying you? Are your feelings changing because something is really not right for you in the relationship? Tell her. Whatever speed bump you hit needs to be discussed between you. She will appreciate your openness and directness. You, in turn, should do everything you can to be gentle and kind—but not to the point of failing to say what needs to be said.

By the way, the complexity surrounding these kinds of issues is perfect material to sort out with your coach. That's the person who has the expertise, training, and objectivity to help you see past a blind spot. Your coach can help you see the lessons if you've missed them. Maybe you heard mild or loving suggestions from your partner as devastating criticism. Or you have been too demanding, too aggressive, too picky, too preoccupied, unkind, or who knows what. Your coach will spot these things and mirror them for you so you can understand them.

If it is time to break up, and especially if you are both aware and sensitive people, the split may be hard. Generating hard feelings as you leave makes it easier to move on but leaves damage in your wake. Better that you call on every skill you have to avoid making a mess.

DEPARTURE STRATEGY

Bring things to a close by arranging to meet her for lunch or dinner in a safe, neutral, not too intimate public place where neither of you will feel cornered. (What worked best for me was to start the discussion over a meal and then continue it during a walk in a beautiful place, where we could easily, and with no worry about her physical safety, go our separate ways. It wasn't until we were walking that I would tell her, kindly, how final my decision was.)

As you drop the bomb, you'll want to say as many positive things as you can. By your actions and by what you say, make it clear that you are not cold, unfeeling, and thinking only of yourself. Nor is she a bad person. It's just that the relationship is not working and one of you has to be the messenger. Convey the thought that everyone is different with different people, and it's obvious the chemistry between you isn't building the green you both deserve.

Find at least three things you can *truthfully* tell her. For instance:

- Tell her you've had a wonderful time getting to know her. Reminisce about the good times you've had together.
- Mention her good points and things about her that you appreciate.
- Tell her how those qualities have made you feel.
- You might mention her children, parents, or friends and how much you like them.
- Discuss what you have learned from her while you have been together.

Then bring the conversation around to the close:

- Tell her that although she is one of the most interesting (or intelligent, funny, lively, fun, beautiful, thoughtful) people you have ever met, the relationship doesn't really fit for you.
- Give her some examples to illustrate what doesn't fit; show how, no matter how hard you both have worked on the issues, the issues persist.
- Conclude with some more truthful, *positive* observations, including where she has been right in the relationship and perhaps you have been slow, unwilling, or unable to respond.

Kindness is important here. Even if she agrees with you, this is a hard discussion. Allow for some bad feelings on her part, and perhaps yours, too. Be aware that anger may be waiting in the wings to finish breaking up the relationship for you. But anger can quickly turn ugly and give both of you the wrong kind of "permission" to end the relationship. Your skill level has to be good enough to handle her anger without your becoming angry or aggressive. That is not to say you should project a phony or superior calm—just stay as balanced as you can and don't match or escalate her anger. Bring things to a close with as little damage to each other as possible. (It would be best to preview your skills with your coach if you see the breakup coming.)

Stay in charge of yourself—minimize anger at every opportunity. Don't allow it to build beyond what is absolutely necessary to support your leaving the relationship. Handle this time as though neither of you is guilty of anything. You both did your best, but you both need to move on. Neither of you will find what you're looking for by delaying the inevitable. In friendship, help her to let go and hope she allows you the same courtesy. Think of the relationship *and* the reasons for the breakup as another learning experience on the way to your goal.

Certain deep residual feelings between you may never be resolved or forgotten, so don't expect that you can call her in a month or even a year to find out how she's doing. A friendly parting is the most you can expect, regardless of how she treats you. Hold her in your heart as you leave. Know that if she treats you badly now, it's because she doesn't have the emotional control to separate without blaming you. *She's acting that way so she'll feel less pain in parting.*

In any case, you don't have to match her energy. Back away as gracefully as possible. "I'm sorry, it doesn't work," is enough. Again: cast no blame, and resist any urge to defend yourself or make her wrong. She will appreciate your style later on.

SOME EXAMPLES OF GRACEFUL EXITS

Leaving shorter relationships. Tell her something like this on the phone or in person: "I've enjoyed meeting you [being with you] and you're really a lovely person. But I don't think I've dated enough to begin an exclusive relationship, and I want to be open about that. So thank you very much for everything, and I wish you well."

If you wanted to keep the friendship, you might include: "I've been thinking about our relationship. We're probably better as friends than as a couple."

Leaving longer relationships. This conversation needs to take place in person. "I treasure our friendship and who you are, but I think we both need to move on. We've been together for six months [almost a year, two years], and I notice that we're still struggling with issues that we just can't seem to resolve. I know you would like our relationship to be easier by now, and so would I. This is really difficult, but I don't think we have reason to hope for more. I think the kindest thing is for us both to move on."

Whether she's angry, sad, taken off-guard, or whatever, just listen to her, and agree with her as much as you can. *After she's said it all* (allow her to empty without disagreeing or interrupting!), tell her what has disappointed you and what you've loved about your relationship. Restate your position—you want to move on—in as loving and considerate a way as possible. There is no need to make her wrong. If it's truthful, tell her, "I'm so sorry. I think we were a very good step-along-the-way for one another. We've both gained a lot from being with each other."

And you might even be surprised: She may be enormously relieved.

INTO THE FUTURE

So you love her. So you love how you feel and act when you're *with* her. So you want to build something together. You're ready for Section IV.

Its two chapters explore the adventure of a new relationship—after that wonderful moment when you pass the point of no return. They offer a frank discussion about the effects of money on your relationship and whether the M word is for you.

Are you ready? Read on!

"*I'm sorry if my income is hurtful to you.*"

Although gold dust is precious,
when it gets in your eyes it obstructs your vision.
—Hsi-Tang

13

YOUR MONEY OR YOUR LIFE (TOGETHER)

A FRANK DISCUSSION

You've found her. She's more than a companion—she is your loverand best friend. Things are just as exciting as when you were twenty. You're ready to pop the question because you're so convinced she's the one. Yet you can't help noticing that you haven't been open with each other in one critical area: money.

Sex is a deal-breaker, and so are assets or the lack of them. Because of that, more marriages get in trouble over finances than over sex. So, if you want a closer, more open and trusting relationship with her, you'll have to "open the books." It's another way to get to know each other. Nobody likes negative surprises, so disclosure *now* will maintain the vital trust between you. If serious losses arise because either of you has concealed a financial dilemma, no amount of romantic feelings will keep your mutual trust from being damaged.

And there is good reason to have left this subject for last: It's dangerous.

Short of dishonesty, there is probably no right or wrong approach to the subject of money. The public's desire for even more than 31 flavors of ice cream is simple testimony to how we can all be different and still be "right." The same with couples and money—you can each have different values and still be right. Your task is to discover what works for both of you, what you're both comfortable with, and how you're going to live from now on compared with how you've lived in the past. Pick a flavor you can both agree on and go for it.

In the first marriage, assets probably were not a significant issue. You both had dreams and plans, but because you didn't have any money, you concentrated on getting just enough into your checking account to fulfill them. Children and career were priorities as you built your future. But the handling of money, income, finances, and property is nearly always an issue in a second marriage, because now you *have* money, income, finances, and property—maybe even lots of it.

In a midlife marriage, partners reap the rewards of having lived a lot. They each have their own preexisting economic priorities, and there are more voices in the chorus—children, parents, you, me, and many others—singing out for recognition. So, there's a lot to consider.

What follows are some nitty-gritty questions that need more than answers. They require agreement—which means that even though *you* are sorely tempted to make the rules, the two of you must come to an understanding without either of you feeling coerced. So:

1. What is your net worth, and what is hers?
2. What is your income, and what is hers?
3. What is her credit-card debt and tax liability, and what is yours?
4. If houses are involved, whose house are you going to live in, and what will be done with the other one?
5. How are you going to handle your checking and savings accounts? Will you keep them separate? Combine them?
6. Are you in agreement about borrowing and credit cards—about how much is okay and how much is too much?
7. What is a comfortable level of discretionary spending—over what period of time?
8. Who is going to manage the monthly bills?
9. Who is going to police the problem of excess spending?
10. Who pays for whose children's education?

11. Who is going to pay for the care of whose aging parents?
12. What kind of health insurance are you going to have, and who will provide it?
13. How do you work out issues related to alimony and/or child support if there has been a divorce?
14. If one of you dies, how will the estate be distributed?

We all understand that financial agreement must be reached if our lives are to work smoothly. And these lives of ours are complicated. We—my lover/spouse and I—are different. Our children are different—maybe one is a brain surgeon and another is a drug addict. How do we handle the financial aspects of that? How do we fund and leave money to these kids? Premarital (also known as prenuptial) agreements can do the job. Premarital agreements are contracts, and like any contract, there's a "handshake," then a written agreement to memorialize what the handshake was about. This means you must figure out what you both want to do and then have a contract engineer (transactional lawyer) say it for you on paper.

PREMARITAL AGREEMENTS

Premarital agreements exist for any number of reasons, including:

1. To simplify the untangling of your financial relationship should your marriage not work out.
2. To protect you financially from your partner's children and your children from their new stepparent.
3. To protect you as a couple from the outside world, such as each other's prior tax liabilities and credit-card debt.
4. To keep you from having to rehash all the negative financial stuff. Hashing it out once was enough.
5. To remove the incentive for either of you to be marrying for the wrong reasons. If the relationship is going to blow up over money, you'd be better off to have that happen at the prenup stage than after you're married.
6. To help your partner recognize that she has a decent parachute should her five years with you not turn into six. Remember, that the years she has invested in the marriage were an asset she

contributed—time is money. That investment deserves to be recognized should the relationship short-circuit.

My idea of a premarital agreement is one that, in most cases, doesn't last forever. It self-destructs after five—or, at the most, ten—years. Most family lawyers I know evaluate your net worth, income, complexity of your estate, and the disparity of your net worth. If one or both of you is beyond a certain threshold, the lawyer will urge you to enter a premarital agreement to formalize your earlier handshake on the financial issues.

Whether a formal agreement is necessary is up to you. You have to consider how much financial baggage (good or bad) you have accumulated and the extent of the economic disparity between you. If you're marrying someone who shares a similar economic status, you might not need a formal agreement. If the marriage blows up, each of you will simply fall back on what you had before the union and go on. However, the need for a formal agreement is a lot different if one of you has accumulated assets greatly in excess of the other's prior to the marriage.

If you're the one short on assets you'd better believe that finances are on her mind. If you are honorable about the marriage and the financial disparity between you, and the subject has not come up, you might bring it up yourself by mentioning that you are willing to sign a premarital agreement. In your discussion, you could say that a marital partnership probably needs five years to mellow before it can be regarded as financially stable. Therefore an agreement—for at least five years—to protect what she has accumulated would be in order. Whether she wants the agreement or not, trust between you will soar. Finances are now a non-issue, so you can deal more freely with the other "stuff" between you. And that makes those issues easier to resolve.

On the other hand, if you're the one with the significant assets, you definitely need to understand certain things. Money not only represents but *is* power and freedom. Going into "survival mode" is human nature when your power or your freedom are threatened. When people fear being left with little or nothing at the end of a marriage, they feel powerless and will "go to war" to restore their sense of self. So the message is that things will most likely get ugly if (1) you have assets greatly in excess of your partner's, (2) you have no premarital agreement, *and* (3) the marriage dissolves. When love goes out the window, money flies in. Count on it—especially if you've got big money.

AVOIDING WRITTEN AGREEMENTS—MAYBE

If large amounts of money and/or substantial property holdings are not involved, a formal written agreement can sometimes be avoided if assets are brought together in stages. The story of how Bill and Joan proceeded is an excellent example of this.

As they grew closer in their dating and premarital experience, they discussed most of the fourteen questions at the beginning of this chapter and found comfortable solutions.

They each agreed to initially retain what they had accumulated separately. They decided that, as the marriage grew, they would allow their assets to blend slowly—which is what assets tend to do naturally anyway. While they trusted each other absolutely, they also recognized that second marriages can fail for unforeseen reasons and that sudden business reversals could wipe out both estates. They wanted time—about five years—to come together as a couple, to make their lives physically and emotionally stable, before they brought their finances together. As long as they did not *commingle* (merge) their assets, there would be no argument over who owned what. Other states may differ, but in California, if an asset is kept separate and identifiable (not commingled), it remains the separate property of its owner. Therefore, if Bill and Joan had to undo their marriage, they would need only to agree on how to split the community assets they had acquired while together. With that handled, they could go on with their lives, taking their separate property with them without controversy.

The couple agreed to live in Bill's home. They decided to sell Joan's family home when the market was right. Until she sold her house, she made payments on it from the proceeds of her late husband's life insurance, since those were also her separate property.

Joan and Bill kept separate checking and savings accounts containing their individual cash assets. They decided to use his income to cover their living expenses and to build their savings out of hers. Even though they were both living in Bill's home, he maintained the home, his business, and other investments as his separate property. Most of

Bill's earnings from the business were contributed to pay for all of their expenses, income taxes, and most of Joan's discretionary spending. Joan's entire income from her professional livelihood went into their newly-opened joint *savings* account. All of Joan's investment income remained her separate property. Occasionally, she would resort to her investment income to cover additional discretionary spending.

When Joan sold her house, the proceeds were deposited in her separate savings account and later into investment accounts comprised of mutual funds held in her name.

Four or five years later they felt very comfortable putting everything together. She initiated the idea by transferring her investment accounts into community property accounts that were held in both of their names. Bill did the same with his accounts and deeded Joan a common interest in all of his real estate and businesses for her to hold in community property with him. They had delayed commingling their assets until they were really comfortable with their marriage. That doesn't mean the marriage was without disagreement and occasional disputes—it does mean that the marriage was without serious flaws.

Then, a surprise. All of their children simultaneously announced that they wanted to go to graduate school. This translated into many, many thousands of dollars each for school and the associated living expenses. Their timing was understandable; there was a major downturn in the economy, and the job market was depressed and depressing—but so was Bill's and Joan's income during this period. They resolved the problem by dividing the responsibility for the children's additional years of education between themselves and each child. The children each took a loan for their schooling. The parents agreed to pay for the children's living expenses out of his business. When those funds fell short, Joan took the rest out of the joint savings that she had been storing away as her part of the deal.

Bill's and Joan's mothers were still alive at this time. Her mother was self-funding, and Bill's was in a very expensive "inn" for the aged. The latter's expenses were paid out of Bill's business income. When Joan's mother died, Joan received an inheritance which was placed in community property, although Joan handled the investment of those funds.

Eventually, their income and investments grew and prospered. Joan and Bill found that each half of the community property was worth a lot more than before they brought their separate finances together. Any financial disparity between them had been obliterated.

Bill and Joan have been together for twelve years. They love their three children—each is a unique and beautiful addition to their family. There is, of course that special feeling for blood, but it has become insignificant. Each child is fully accepted into the new family, and if something happens to Bill or Joan, all the funds are in a family trust. That trust goes to the surviving spouse, and when the survivor dies, the residual in the trust will be paid to all three children equally.

For your information, I have included a formal premarital agreement as Appendix B. Everyone has heard about premarital agreements, but few people have ever seen one. Page through the agreement now, even if you don't read it closely. You will get a sense of what it contains and what is important. Notice that the agreement is a formal presentation of the information you and your beloved want to generally disclose to one another. I'm not suggesting that you either do or don't see a lawyer. I am suggesting that you be cautious—and comfortable with your decision. You could regard the story of how Bill and Joan handled things as all very nice for them, but their solution might not suit you or interest you at all.

The discussion of money may also bring to light previously unrecognized differences in values and priorities between partners. Consider the issue of a home for the newlyweds. Whose house are you going to live in? Are you selling one and moving into the other—or selling both? I have a friend who wanted to sell both houses and scale down to a condo on a golf course. His bride, he discovered, wanted to scale up and have a gracious home with marble floors so she could entertain family, friends, and grandchildren and have everyone sleep over. The moral: Don't presume that what you want is the only picture in the album.

People in their fifties often have parents who are becoming old and infirm. You had better know if your new wife pictures her mother living with you in the event that Mom is unable to take care of herself. If money is short, *you* will be paying for her mother's care. In addition, if elderly people are in your lives, and you have an idea that you're going to get married and run off to Tahiti to build a dream house, calm your greedy gland right now—it probably ain't gonna happen.

Discretionary money and discretionary time are another consideration. Every individual must have some money and time to call his or her own without comment from a curious spouse. If your wife has only a dollar a week of discretionary money and she saves it so she can buy two twenty-five dollar lipsticks at the end of the year, that is none of your business. She also has a right to pursue interests that you don't understand or share at all. It's not fair to hover. Leave her alone—and absolutely make no cute comments. Discretionary time and money are a private matter.

As we age, we view finances differently than when we were younger. When women move into midlife, they often become as interested in financial issues as men were early on. As your new spouse grows older, she might want to realize her long-time dream of opening a bookstore at the mall. Then you come along and say, "I'm ready to cut back on work. I want a playmate, and I don't want you making commitments that confine us. What do you mean you want a new career? Do you really think I want my wife stuck in a bookstore all day?"

Stop and think. You might be asking your wife to give up building her nest egg and nurturing her dream. If she agrees, that entitles her to ask you to protect her from the financial demands of her later years. She wants to take greater financial responsibility, while you say, "Just come and play with me." So, you will need to set aside funds to cover—very generously—what would have been her income, should your marriage terminate through death or divorce. Or you must adjust to her opening a bookstore. Be ready for this issue as we move forward in the new millennium. Many women are increasingly interested in protecting themselves and maintaining a professional identity outside the home.

MEGA-DISPARITY—CAN IT WORK?

What happens if the woman—your love—has mega-more money than you do? What if she is a physician's widow with a net worth of three million dollars? Or what happens if you earn $15,000 a year as an artist, and you fall in love with a woman who makes $25,000 a day in oil? (True story.) Can this marriage work?

Maybe you are fiercely proud and dread not living up to your own expectations, so you don't want her to pay for your expenses regardless of how different your income levels are. Such a stand can cause a pinch in the relationship. Maybe she likes to go first-class and you can't afford that. To make this marriage work, you'll want to base your status in the relationship on something more consequential than money. You will also want to have a good sense of yourself, work that matters to you, and something that validates you as a man in your own eyes as well as in hers. Can you see that a premarital agreement would be a good idea because of the financial disparity here? Otherwise, you can end up feeling like she's buying you rather than joining you in a relationship.

A man might refuse to marry a woman with money because he doesn't want to feel diminished, even though the woman has no desire to diminish him. Nevertheless, in midlife a man wants to be challenged less and admired more. He wants to be able to look into the eyes of his love and see an improved reflection of himself.

Whatever your situation, if it is troublesome, it's time for a coach. Your problems are not new—to many professionals these are old wrinkles that have been smoothed out many times. The right financial advisor and therapist/coach can put you two on the map. If this woman is your true love, you can't say, "I'm sorry—you're too rich" (or too old or too anything). You just talk to your advisors and mature into the challenge.

PLANS PAY OFF

For all I've said about money, the central subject is still "trust." If you don't trust her, it's time to run. Now! If you do trust her, it's time to open the books and anticipate any difficulties that lie ahead. Treat your finances like a road map—both of you follow an agreed-upon financial route to get there from here. You need a plan you can implement if there is a divorce or death or illness or total disability—or if, God forbid, the IRS makes a game of your life's work.

Suppose she becomes ill and her children oppose what you're doing to care for their mother, and they ask that you not make decisions for her anymore. If things get rough, they'll ask why you're spending so much money and what you're spending it on. You'll be shocked and resent them for interfering. Imagine how wonderful it would be to have your property and income clearly parceled out between the two of you and/or to have a premarital agreement to protect you from her children.

This is only a wake-up chapter. Actually, an entire book on the subject would be needed to do justice to the discussion of money, income, finances, and property between couples. A number of impressive and helpful works have been written by acknowledged experts. Among them are *Couples & Money: A Couples' Guide Updated for the New Millenium,* by Victoria Felton-Collins, Ph.D., CFP, and Suzanne Blair Brown (Gabriel Books, 1998) and *Remarriage and Your Money: Once Again, For Richer or Poorer,* by Patricia Schiff Estess (Little, Brown & Co., 1992).

Face it: Deep down you want your true love to save you the embarrassment of having to bring up all the things I've covered in this chapter. You'd love her even more if she would put all her cards on the table first. She may not know how to do that. Regardless, you can bet the issue is as much on her mind as it is on yours. At least it should be.

Money isn't happiness, but neither is it a dirty word. It's a medium of exchange that's necessary for survival, and if you can't talk about it, you don't have enough trust to go forward in the relationship. Forward—as in the other M word. . . .

HIS

"And do you, Rebecca, promise to make love only to Richard, month after month, year after year, and decade after decade, until one of you is dead?"

HERS

"I had a nice time, Steve. Would you like to come in, settle down, and raise a family?"

A single man . . . is an incomplete animal.
He resembles the odd half of a pair of scissors.
— Benjamin Franklin

14

THE M WORD
MORE OF EVERYTHING

Why marriage?

I think we can agree that men and women each form partially overlapping halves of the human equation. We are complementary opposites who become spiritually complete by joining the fullness of our halves together. Even though it is perfectly normal to remain unmarried (the unmarried state has its own pleasures and pains), a good marriage fulfills our soul's longing for "more."

Whether or not marriage is involved, every relationship destined for intimacy goes from one step to the next. If one of you can't take the next step, the relationship fades and disappears in a flurry of blame, guilt, and meaningless reasons.

Even though the institution of marriage has had some bad press, how you experience anything, including marriage, depends on you. You know what it means to be married and can judge for yourself whether it's something you want to risk again. Whatever you decide, marriage asks you and your partner to give up certain aspects of the single life. You're ready to do that if you've been growing—if you know, or you've learned, that each of you must give in order to receive, that you must water and nurture the seeds that will become your future.

This book presumes you have lost the person with whom you once shared your heart in marriage and that you have begun to think about marrying again. The purpose of this chapter is to help you consider remarrying from your wiser, more mature perspective. No matter what, if you choose to marry again, you can count on it being a very different experience. You're older. You've already reached a variety of personal and professional plateaus. You are more now, and that "more" can make a big difference to you both. The new woman in your life will have needs and desires quite different from those of the girl you married the first time out, not only because she's a different person but because she is a more grown-up person. You have a chance to try again, to succeed, to fulfill your dream of finding a woman who is full of love and looking for a partner just like you to help make her life happen in a whole new wonderful way. But, you ask, is getting married again really worth the trouble?

Not only have you and your lady matured, but so has our society. It has shifted its perspective on marriage and on the "place" of the man and woman in it. Marriage used to be what we all were "supposed" to do. But now both sexes have more freedom to weigh their options. That raises a logical question: Since people are relatively free these days to live together in an unmarried state, why take the big leap? "After all," we're told, "getting married doesn't really change anything." The truth is, marriage changes *everything*.

You are building a relationship upon increasing levels of commitment, sensitivity, and awareness. At each level you are laying the foundation for the next level of intimacy—the next stage of your relationship. The marriage ceremony itself is but one stage—and hardly the final one.

LEVELS OF INTIMACY

Here are some of the steps that an intimate relationship can go through—although not necessarily in this order—as it approaches and moves beyond the marriage ceremony:

1. Meeting and interviewing one another
2. Meeting again to see if it's worth your time and emotional involvement
3. Dating
4. Sex
5. Developing a history with each other
6. Learning to handle each other's "junk"
7. Building deeper layers of trust
8. Longing for more, planning for the future
9. The M word
10. The engagement period—planning for the big day
11. The ceremony
12. The honeymoon
13. Sexy and sweet—a wonderful new reality
14. The new reality becomes routine—a day-to-day affair—and you love it
15. Finding Agape, the deep love—discovering your own subtle new feelings
16. Deepening the relationship
17. Discovering that "Every day I want to marry you again. You are so beautiful, and I love who I am in your eyes. How can we go even deeper than this? And then deeper? And deeper still?"
18. Previously rare moments of ecstasy grow more frequent

If the relationship doesn't reach toward—and find—deeper, more satisfying levels, then it isn't growing. The truth is, Eros always dies, while Agape nourishes a lifetime of expanding, deeper, lasting love. Nothing stands still in life; something is either growing or it's dying. Staying trapped in old patterns is easy regardless of how much pain it causes. But this disease of the status quo obscures our imagination, discourages us from fulfilling each other's dreams, and it promises that the relationship will flatline.

It's reassuring to know that wonderful, extremely satisfying new levels of intimacy follow marriage. These are complex, multi-layered experiences that can't be accessed without that public declaration of personal commitment, because neither of you will relax and fully surrender into the green until you have finally and irrevocably committed to each other.

Times and people have changed. Couples have changed as well. Why not be part of the grand adventure of redefining marriage?

CHANGING TIMES: THE MEANING OF PARTNERSHIP

Marriage as *partnership* is an important concept for couples. The opposite of partnership is domination. Domination doesn't work in your life, so why should it work in hers? As two wings are required to fly, genuine liberation results from the surrender of each whole person to the other. Unless you both give, you can't get, can't grow, and can't build—and any chance you have at ecstasy and bliss will elude you.

Thirty years ago great numbers of women began to demand "equality," not only in terms of equal opportunity in the business world, but in their personal lives as well. Men would want nothing less for themselves. When you think clearly about it, the true liberation of men actually *depends* upon women being liberated (and vice versa). When they are, we gain our other half with all her power, courage, and ability.

Social and personal equality doesn't mean exchanging male dominance for female dominance. Neither does it mean a woman wants you to be less masculine or that you want her to be less feminine. Equality means both of you are freed up to develop some of the qualities of the opposite sex in yourselves. As a man, you're freed up to *feel* more (developing your feminine aspect), and she's freed up to *do* more (developing her masculine aspect). Each of you then has a much greater "self" and, therefore, a lot more to bring to the relationship. "Who's on top?" is no longer important, because you are now whole partners—side by side.

Personally, I prefer having a partner, not a subordinate, to fill out my life, a partner to laugh and plan with. I am supercharged by the feelings generated by commitment to a person who is my complementary opposite. I want what she can add to my life. I want to feel life with her—its agony and its ecstasy—and I don't want to miss anything. "Who I am" shows up best when I'm married to my equal—my partner.

Partnership means we're committed. We each pull together, but in our own style. We make different, but equally important, contributions to our relationship. *Women want, and deserve, partnership where each person can give and be given to, can love and be loved in return, and both partners can be emotionally healed through kindness, consideration, and understanding. Why would men want, or deserve, any less?*

PARTNERSHIP AND ROMANCE

You can make great memories as your relationship deepens. Invest in the relationship emotionally and financially. Come together with style and a flourish that you'll both remember with a sentimental smile in the years to come. Buy her flowers. Send her cards and leave her love notes. Picnic on a beautiful lawn, a hillside, a private beach, or in the woods by a waterfall. Surprise her. How about some sourdough bread and cheese with a carefully selected wine—shared intimately at your favorite spot to sit and dream? Feel the special glow you share. Watch the sky, hold hands, and tell her what you love about her and how she makes you feel.

Don't forget to include tickets to the performing arts. Dinner followed by a special evening at the theater or a concert will be long remembered, and the elegant atmosphere will put you both in a romantic light.

Find a special hideaway where you can return to renew your hearts in the years to come. Call ahead for flowers to welcome her. Give her romance. *As you are drawn to pictures of beautiful women, she is drawn to romantic stories. Let her be your picture of a beautiful woman—while you fulfill her need for storybook romance.* If you're not sure what's romantic, take a look at *A Thousand and One Ways to Be Romantic,* by Gregory J. P. Godek (Sourcebooks Trade, 1999).

MAKE HER SAFE—AND WATCH

By this time in your life, I hope you've learned that "Let me be the one you love" is needy and boring. Rather, "Let me love you" is what mysteriously works. Again, I want to remind you that sex is different from love. Your relationship is built on love, caring, and affection. Without those, sex builds nothing.

Building begins as you become mutual caretakers—stewards of each other's well-being (as in making sure she takes her vitamin pills and gets nourishment, enough rest, and affection).

The most important thing you can give each other is *love*—not sex.

Then mix in some sex for the fun of it and to deepen the experience of your union.

IS IT TIME?

"To everything there is a season," and every relationship has a rhythm. If you pay attention, there's a moment when "the M word" is a sweet elephant in the living room. Feed the elephant and it will grow bigger and happier, ignore it and it will wreak havoc in your relationship.

You have a period of time within which your lady reasonably expects you to ask her to marry you. When her expectations are ignored, she begins to subconsciously protect herself from rejection by withdrawing to emotional safety. In other words, she will start building walls, and somehow your relationship will feel it.

Think of it this way: If you're playing tennis and complimenting your opponent on great shots, and your opponent never reciprocates, after a while you naturally withdraw and go into a different mode with that person. If you fail to compliment others in the workplace, you cannot expect them to give you their very best work and their unstinting loyalty.

Like you, a woman wants to be complimented for the fullness of who she is in your life. The ultimate—and, at a certain point in your relationship, the only acceptable—compliment is "Will you marry me?" or words to that effect. Only then does she have a tangible stake in the future you're both working toward.

Compliments *validate* us and what we're doing. If we are never complimented or openly appreciated, it's natural for us to invalidate ourselves. If you don't ask her to marry you within a reasonable window of time, your silence translates into a loud rejection. There are consequences for that. So you need either to validate and empower your partner or move on to another relationship.

What's "a reasonable window of time"? I'd say you have approximately two years before Eros wears off and your relationship deepens and becomes more subtle with the onset of Agape. Why wait until the pizzazz of Eros is gone? Why wait until you have passed her window of expectation? Why wait until she's held her smile for so long that it freezes? Keep the relationship strong and enthusiastic. Take the risk—seize the moment and ask her to marry you as soon as you know it's time. As Dr. Susan Jeffers would say, "Feel the fear and do it anyway."

Are you thinking that you don't want to marry again? Well, you can't build anything together without her snuggling in and committing to you, and I don't know how that's possible without you doing the same. Without a commitment, each of you naturally has a lingering doubt and one foot near the door.

By now you know who you're looking for. Be careful, and look in deep, gentlemen. "Seekers" notoriously seek—and having found . . . they seek on. They seek on past their goal—over and over again. By the time they realize their mistake, the jewel has already been scooped up. Marriage is the time-tested solution, the most productive way to position yourself for a life of ever-expanding love accompanied by continued personal growth and prosperity.

It's time to follow your heart—to use what you have learned here to find and settle in with your other half and say, "Come, be with me, my love . . . hold my hand and dream."

TED'S AND DIANA'S EPILOGUES

His: This book is filled with thoughts, insights, and strategies gathered over more than forty years of relationships. They reflect who I became as I lived beyond the loss of Sharon, my first wife and the mother of my children.

It is said that Paris, once known, remains forever in our hearts, and so it is with the great loves we've shared. Such indelible experiences nurture our souls and endow who we are, just as future relationships serve to add new depth and fresh beauty to our past. They make us more than we've ever been before. *So it's not unfaithful for us to treasure our sweet memories nor is it disloyal to move forward to fill our impoverished hearts.*

Diana and I are grateful to Paul (her first husband) and Sharon for having housebroken us so well. Most likely we would not have been such a wonderful surprise to one another if they hadn't shaped us with their love.

If you've been housebroken, molded, and shaped too, I can only hope that the strategies and insights collected here will bring you the success and fulfillment that I've enjoyed. We are all so different, and there are many stories with happy endings. I wish you the best version of your own.

Hers: The first qualities I loved in Ted were his humor, his aliveness, and his clarity about what he had to offer in a relationship and what he required in return. He had really done his homework—by the time I came along he had spent two years "interviewing" or dating many women, knowing that each was either his "goal" or the lesson he was determined to learn before he could find the perfect lady to share his future with.

When we met over twelve years ago, we just clicked. It didn't bother me a bit that I was number 131 on his *Rate-a-Date* software! I loved how he had thought through and smoothed the bumps of our coming together in midlife.

Now I marvel at how our relationship grows deeper and sweeter every year. Both our lives are better and easier for having joined together.

APPENDIX A

FAMILIARIZING YOURSELF WITH STDS: THE DETAILS

We can't trust luck when 15 million new cases of sexually transmitted diseases are recorded every year in the United States (we are rapidly approaching a time when one in four citizens, male and female, will be a carrier). The good news is that most of these diseases are curable; the bad news is that people often aren't diagnosed—either because they don't have any symptoms or because they don't recognize certain symptoms as related to an STD—so the diseases are easily and unknowingly passed along from partner to partner.

The most frequently encountered STDs can be divided into two classifications: (1) bacterial and viral, and (2) curable and incurable. The common bacterial STDs are curable, and damage is minimal if diagnosed early on. The most common viral STDs are not curable, though they may go into remission.

BACTERIAL STDs

Chlamydia. Curable. Highly transmittable—it is, in fact, the most common bacterial STD. Symptoms develop between four and twenty-eight days following intercourse with an infected partner. Only 60 percent of infected men will have symptoms: painful, burning urination; and clear or cloudy fluid discharge from the penis. Eighty percent of infected women have no symptoms. Women who do have symptoms will experience abdominal pain with painful urination, painful intercourse, and discharge of yellow mucus and pus from the vagina. Engaging in oral or anal sex when infected will, in turn, infect the throat or rectum and result in a purulent (pus-like) discharge from the infected area.

Chlamydia is treated with common antibiotics. Failure to treat it results in scarring of the lining of the testes (epididymis) and the urethra. The scarring of the urethra will serve to permanently obstruct urine flow and may result in painful erection and intercourse. For women, there are long-term consequences, including the risk of scarring the fallopian tubes, which can result in infertility, pelvic inflammatory disease, or ectopic pregnancy.

Trichomoniasis. Curable. Highly transmittable. Symptoms appear two to six days after exposure. In men, symptoms show up as a pus-like discharge from the penis with painful urination accompanied by the need to urinate frequently. Often the symptoms are so mild that they are neither felt nor recognized as a problem. In women, the symptoms are more apparent than in men: there is obvious inflammation and swelling of the genitalia and intercourse is painful. Treatment requires *both* infected partners to be orally medicated simultaneously.

Gonorrhea. Curable. Highly transmittable. In men, symptoms appear from two to seven days after exposure. Purulent discharge from the penis is accompanied by pain in the urethra, with frequency and urgency in urination. The penile opening often reddens and swells. In women, symptoms appear seven to twenty-one days after exposure. Frequency and urgency in urination and purulent discharge are accompanied by pain and perhaps fever. Her symptoms are typically not as dramatic as the male's and therefore may remain untreated for months; this causes her to unknowingly spread the infection to her partner(s). Oral or anal sex with an infected partner can infect the throat or rectum. If not treated immediately, the infection can spread through the bloodstream and seriously affect the skin, heart, liver, and joints. Treatment consists of an injection of antibiotics followed by a week of oral antibiotics, unless the infection has reached the blood; if it has, hospitalization for intravenous antibiotics is required. Urethritis (painful inflammation of the urinary tube between the bladder and the tip of the penis) may reoccur as post-gonococcal urethritis and become more difficult to treat.

Syphilis. Curable. Highly transmittable. The bacterium enters the body through mucous membranes at the penile opening, vagina, or mouth, or through the skin. After two or three weeks—but perhaps as many as thirteen weeks—a sore or ulcer (technically, a chancre—pronounced "shanker") is seen at the infection site, typically involving the reproductive organs, mouth, or anus. The sore leaks a clear fluid that is highly infectious. The sore is low-grade, heals in a few weeks, and is easily ignored, because the disease is carried in the blood throughout the body and becomes "second stage." Syphilis is justly famous—and feared—for its insidious, pernicious damage to the body, nervous system, and organs, including heart, brain, stomach, bladder, and reproductive organs. If you think there is a chance you have syphilis, see a doctor immediately. Treatment: penicillin. But a cure may not be that easy; listen to your doctor and read about the disease and what can be done about it.

VIRAL STDs

Hepatitis B. Sometimes not curable. Low transmission rate. Preventable by vaccination before exposure. Onset of symptoms occurs forty days to six months after exposure. After exposure, treatment with human immune globulin might protect you from infection. This virus is transmitted between sexual partners through bodily secretions or blood, or between drug users through sharing hypodermic needles. It inflames the liver and causes fever, nausea and vomiting, and loss of appetite. While it can be fatal, it usually runs its course in eight weeks or less. In approximately 5 to 10 percent of victims, chronic (not curable) liver infection occurs leading to permanent liver damage and possibly cancer of the liver. Victims infected with chronic hepatitis B are 100 times more likely to develop liver cancer than persons without Hepatitis B virus in their blood.

Hepatitis C. Not curable. Low transmission rate. This is the newest STD to be recognized by the Centers for Disease Control. No vaccine had been announced as of this book's publication. Transmittable from blood to blood. Menstrual blood can contain the virus. Common symptoms are extreme tiredness, itching, and joint pain. The disease process is slow and, unless it goes into remission, gradually progresses until it damages the liver. The symptoms are low grade (not obvious), and in 10 percent of the cases may not be recognized until a liver transplant is necessary. It is apparently transmittable even after it goes into remission.

Herpes. Not curable. Variable transmission rate. Herpes simplex virus appears as the type of fever blister we commonly see on someone's lip. When it appears on the genitalia or in the area covered by boxer shorts, it's called genital herpes. While the virus can be transmitted at any stage of the outbreak, it is most transmittable when the blister's fluid leaks out. It is not likely to be transmitted, especially in people over forty, unless there is an outbreak. If your partner is the one who's infected, *usually* she will know when an outbreak is imminent, because it is preceded by a burning, tingling, itching soreness at the site of the impending blister. If she is not aware of the outbreak, she is unable to warn you, and you are at medium-to-high risk to contract the disease. Outbreaks usually recur in the same area of the genitals, so if she is suspicious that she is experiencing a recurrence, inspect the usual site for a lesion or its beginnings.

Abstinence is the best policy during the outbreak. A condom is totally inadequate to protect the base of the penis and scrotum. If you trust to luck and decide to have sex anyway, washing well afterwards is better than doing nothing. The first attack will be followed by frequent recurrences; however, medical treatment can shorten or reduce the number of outbreaks. Herpes can be treated and remain in remission for years, but, again, *there is no cure.* At the time of this writing, authorities are debating as to whether you can contract the disease if your partner is not experiencing an outbreak. But why not always take the cautious approach? If your lady has herpes, be sure to check with the American Social Health Association (919-361-8488 or www.ashastd.org) or your urologist for the latest information.

Genital warts. Not curable. Low transmission rate. A genital wart first appears one to six months after exposure as a small, red, moist bump that rapidly grows into a wart or small clumps of warts. As they mature, they develop a rough surface that has the appearance of a small cauliflower. On men they can develop anywhere on the shaft of the penis, on the scrotum, around the rectum, or even inside the urethra. They are most often found on the base of the shaft. In women they can be distributed anywhere in or around the vaginal area. Although these warts can be removed, there is a high probability of recurrence. The warts are the result of sexually transmitted human papilloma viruses (HPVs). Such viruses may also be pre-cancerous, meaning they can lead to cancer of the penis, vagina, vulva, mouth, or throat. For more information, check with the National HPV Hotline (919-361-4848 or www.ashastd.org).

HIV/AIDS. Not curable. Low transmission rate. Transmitted during sexual relations with an infected partner. The virus, carried by infected body fluids (blood, semen, vaginal fluid, mother's milk, urine, and possibly saliva), can penetrate mucous membranes of the mouth, vagina, or rectum, or the membrane just inside the penile opening. The likelihood of transmission is increased when the skin or mucous membrane is damaged or torn. While skin or membranes are not easily torn during vaginal intercourse, they can be easily damaged during anal sex, since the anus is not designed to be penetrated and vigorously stimulated.

This is the most ominous and lethal STD, and no protection is absolutely certain to prevent infection. Other than abstinence, the condom is the only preventive measure that's said to work. And as of this writing, the medical experts are not unanimous in believing that a condom offers an adequate barrier against the virus. If you don't already know more than I've told you about AIDS, ask your doctor, read about it, and at least research the ways in which the disease is transmitted, so that you have a solid plan for protecting yourself against it. For more information, call the AIDS Hotline at 1-800-227-8922 or1-800-342-2437, or check their Web site, www.ashastd.org.

OTHER STDS

There are two additional STDs: scabies and pubic lice. While not common, they're worth mentioning.

Scabies. A curable mite infestation that's *easily* transmitted through physical (sexual) contact. The mites cause tiny, itchy, red bumps smaller than a pinhead to erupt where the female has laid eggs beneath the first layer of skin. They establish themselves anywhere on the body except the soles of the feet, and the head and neck. Treatment is similar to that for pubic lice.

Pubic lice. Also known as crab louse or crabs. It's a blood-sucking louse that causes inflammation and itching of the skin and can result in eczema. The infestation is seen as bluish spots at the base of hairs around the pubic and perianal areas and possibly on the hairs of the thighs and abdomen. Like a tick, it is broad and very small, measuring less than two millimeters in length. Its first pair of legs is smaller than the other two pairs, so that under magnification it looks like a crab. The eggs, attached to the base of a pubic hair, hatch in two or three weeks. Treatment for scabies and lice is tolerable and usually accomplished through creams, lotions and shampoos, and thorough laundering of clothing and bedding.

Again, it is *your responsibility* to stay clean sexually. This requires great care on your part. If you were unwittingly contaminated while indulging in some earlier exploit, "I'm sorry" will ring hollow when you've passed an STD to your new life partner. Educate yourself! If you have any reason to imagine you might be carrying an STD, see your doctor immediately.

"A lot of it is just legal mumbo-jumbo."

APPENDIX B

SAMPLE PREMARITAL AGREEMENT

THIS AGREEMENT is made and entered into on <u>January 10, 2000</u>, at <u>Newport Beach, California</u>, by and between <u>ROBERT ALMOST</u>, hereinafter referred to as <u>ROBERT</u>, of <u>Orange County, California</u>, and <u>SHIRLEY MORLEY</u>, hereinafter referred to as <u>SHIRLEY</u>, of <u>Los Angeles County, California</u>, with reference to the following facts and purposes:

A. <u>ROBERT</u> and <u>SHIRLEY</u>, who are presently unmarried, plan to be married to each other on or about <u>February 14, 2005</u>.

B. <u>ROBERT</u> is employed as <u>JACK of ALL TRADES</u> and <u>SHIRLEY</u> is <u>NOT</u> employed. Both are in good health and financially self-supporting.

C. <u>ROBERT</u> and <u>SHIRLEY</u> were formerly married to other persons, but each of such former marriages has been terminated by a final judgment of marriage dissolution. Neither <u>ROBERT</u> nor <u>SHIRLEY</u> has any children.

D. Neither <u>ROBERT</u> nor <u>SHIRLEY</u> now has any right, title, claim, or interest in or to the property, income, or estate of the other by reason of their nonmarital relationship, or otherwise, and neither party is indebted to the other.

E. <u>ROBERT</u> and <u>SHIRLEY</u> desire to make a fair and reasonable disclosure of their respective property and financial obligations, one to the other.

F. The parties intend and desire by this Agreement to (1) define their respective rights in the property they now hold and in that property which they may acquire after marriage, and (2) to avoid those interests which, except for this Agreement, each might acquire after their marriage in the income and property of the other as incidents of their contemplated marriage.

G. Both parties hereto recognize that this Agreement is a premarital agreement as defined in California Family Code Section 1610, and understand and intend that the provisions of this Agreement shall prevail over the provisions of law applicable in the absence of this Agreement.

THEREFORE, for good and valuable consideration, including, without limitation, the mutual promises, conditions, and agreements set forth herein and the contemplated marriage of the parties, the parties agree as follows:

BUILD A BETTER SPOUSE TRAP

1. **Effective Date:** This Agreement shall be and become effective as of the date of the contemplated marriage between the parties, and its effectiveness is expressly conditioned upon such marriage. If, for any reason, and irrespective of fault, the contemplated marriage does not take place, this Agreement will be of no force or effect.

2. **Independent Counsel:** The parties acknowledge and agree that they each have been advised to be represented by separate and independent legal counsel. Both parties have had ample time to hire counsel of their own choosing having first had negotiations for and in preparation of this Agreement. ROBERT warrants and represents that he is and has been represented by PETER H. WERNICKE, Attorney at Law, and a member in good standing of the Bar of the State of California. SHIRLEY warrants and represents that she is and has been represented by COURT B. PURDY, Attorney at Law, and a member in good standing of the Bar of the State of California. The parties acknowledge and agree that they have carefully read this Agreement and that the positions memorialized in the Agreement have been explained fully to them by their respective counsel.

3. **Voluntary and Informed Consent:** The parties further acknowledge and agree that they are fully aware of and understand the contents, legal effect, and consequences of this Agreement, and that they entered into this Agreement voluntarily, free from duress, fraud, undue influence, coercion, or misrepresentations of any kind.

4. **Property and Financial Disclosures:**

   a. A fair and reasonable disclosure of all of ROBERT'S property and financial obligations has been made by him to SHIRLEY, and a list of such property and financial obligations is set forth in Exhibit "A" attached hereto and incorporated herein by this reference. It is understood that the figures and amounts of property and financial obligations set forth in Exhibit "A" are approximate and not necessarily exact, but they are intended to be reasonably accurate and are warranted to be the best estimates of such figures and amounts. SHIRLEY hereby expressly and voluntarily waives any right to disclosure of ROBERT'S property and financial obligations beyond the disclosure provided.

   b. A fair and reasonable disclosure of all of SHIRLEY'S property and financial obligations has been made by her to ROBERT, and a list of such property and financial obligations is set forth in Exhibit "B" attached hereto and incorporated herein by this reference. It is understood that the figures and amounts of property and financial obligations set forth in Exhibit "B" are approximate and not necessarily exact, but they are intended to be reasonably accurate and are warranted to be the best estimates of such figures and amounts. ROBERT hereby expressly and voluntarily waives any right to disclosure of SHIRLEY'S property and financial obligations beyond the disclosure provided.

   c. The parties agree that the foregoing disclosures are not an inducement to enter into this Agreement. ROBERT and SHIRLEY agree that each is willing to enter into this Agreement regardless of the nature or extent of the present or future assets, liabilities, income, or expenses of the other, and regardless of any financial arrangements made for his or her benefit by the other.

5. Rights Incident to Parties' Nonmarital Relationship: <u>ROBERT</u> and <u>SHIRLEY</u> acknowledge and agree that they have not previously entered into any other contract, understanding, or agreement, whether express, implied in fact, or implied in law, with respect to each other's property or earnings, wherever or however acquired or with respect to the support or maintenance of each other. Neither party now has, possesses, or claims any right or interest whatsoever, in law or equity, under the laws of any state, in the present or future property, income or estate of the other, or a right to support, maintenance, or rehabilitation payments of any kind whatsoever from the other by reason of the parties' nonmarital relationship. The parties acknowledge that they each have been advised by their respective counsel on California law respecting nonmarital relationships, and they each agree that neither has any rights and/or obligations arising out of their nonmarital relationship with each.

6. Separate Property Interests in Premarital and Post Marital Assets and Acquisitions:

    a. <u>ROBERT</u> and <u>SHIRLEY</u> agree that all property, including the property set forth in Exhibit "A" belonging to <u>ROBERT</u> at the commencement of their contemplated marriage, and any property acquired by <u>HIM</u> during that marriage by gift, bequest, devise, or descent, shall be and remain his separate property. The parties further acknowledge and agree that all rents, issues, profits, increases, appreciation, and income from the separate property of <u>ROBERT</u>, and any other assets purchased or otherwise acquired with the foregoing proceeds, shall be and remain <u>ROBERT'S</u> separate property. The parties agree that a change in the form of <u>ROBERT'S</u> assets as a result of the sale, exchange, hypothecation, or other disposition of such assets, or a change in form of doing business, shall not constitute any change of property characterization, and such assets shall remain <u>ROBERT'S</u> separate property regardless of any change in form. <u>SHIRLEY</u> shall have no right, title, interest, lien, or claim under the laws of any state in or to any of <u>ROBERT'S</u> separate property assets.

    b. <u>ROBERT</u> and <u>SHIRLEY</u> agree that all property, including the property set forth in Exhibit "B" belonging to <u>SHIRLEY</u> at the commencement of their contemplated marriage, and any property acquired by <u>HER</u> during that marriage by gift, bequest, devise, or descent shall be and remain her separate property. The parties further acknowledge and agree that all rents, issues, profits, increases, appreciation, and income from the separate property of <u>SHIRLEY</u>, and any other assets purchased or otherwise acquired with the foregoing proceeds shall be and remain <u>SHIRLEY'S</u> separate property. The parties agree that a change in the form of <u>SHIRLEY'S</u> assets as a result of the sale, exchange, hypothecation, or other disposition of such assets, or a change in form of doing business, shall not constitute a change of property characterization, and such assets shall remain <u>SHIRLEY'S</u> separate property regardless of any change in form. <u>ROBERT</u> shall have no right, title, interest, lien, or claim under the laws of any state in or to any of <u>SHIRLEY'S</u> separate property assets.

7. Community Efforts in Managing Each Party's Own Separate Property Interests:

    a. The parties acknowledge and agree that <u>ROBERT</u> may devote considerable personal time, skill, service, industry, and effort during their marriage to the investment and management of his separate property and the income therefrom, specifically including, without limitation, <u>ROBERT'S</u> existing or future business career. The parties acknowledge and agree that even though the expenditure of <u>ROBERT'S</u> personal time, skill, service, industry, and effort might constitute or create a community property interest, community property income, or community property asset in the absence of this Agreement, no such community property interest, income, or asset shall be created thereby, and any income, profits, accumulations, appreciation, and increase in value of the separate property of <u>ROBERT</u> during marriage shall be and remain entirely <u>ROBERT'S</u> separate property.

    b. The parties acknowledge and agree that <u>SHIRLEY</u> may devote considerable personal time, skill, service, industry, and effort during their marriage to the investment and management of her separate property and income therefrom. The parties acknowledge and agree that even though the expenditure of <u>SHIRLEY'S</u> personal time, skill, service, industry, and effort might constitute or create a community property interest, community property income, or community property asset in the absence of this Agreement, no such community property interest, income, or asset shall be created thereby, and any income, profits, accumulations, appreciation, and increase in the value of the separate property of <u>SHIRLEY</u> during marriage shall be and remain entirely <u>SHIRLEY'S</u> separate property.

8. Community Efforts in Managing the Other Party's Separate Property Interests: The parties acknowledge and agree that during their marriage, one party may choose to contribute considerable personal time, skill, service, industry, and effort to the investment and management of the other party's separate property and the income thereof. The parties acknowledge and agree that even though any such contribution might constitute or create a community property interest, community property income, or a community property asset in the absence of this Agreement, no such community property interest, income, or asset shall be created thereby. The parties further agree that any such contribution shall not create any other claim, right, lien, or interest whatsoever in favor of the party contributing the personal time, skill, service, industry, and effort in or to the other party's separate property and any income, profits, accumulations, appreciation, and increase in value thereof during the parties' marriage.

9. Separate Property Earnings, Deferred Compensation, and Employee Benefits: The parties agree that any earnings, income, or benefits, no matter their nature, kind, or source, from and after the marriage, including but not limited to salary, bonuses, stock options, deferred compensation, and retirement benefits, shall be the separate property of the party earning or acquiring such earnings, income, or benefits as though the contemplated marriage had never occurred. There shall be no allocation made of any such earnings, income, or benefits between community property and separate property, and such earnings, income or benefits shall

be entirely the separate property of the party earning or acquiring the same. The parties acknowledge their understanding that in the absence of this Agreement, any earnings, income, or benefits resulting from the personal services, skills, industry, and efforts of either party during the contemplated marriage would be community property.

10. Separate Property Interests in Preexisting Retirement and Employee Benefit Plans: ROBERT presently owns a substantial beneficial interest in various retirement benefits, including, but not limited to, a defined benefit pension plan. SHIRLEY acknowledges and agrees that pursuant to the terms of this Agreement, all retirement benefits presently owned by or held for the benefit of ROBERT, together with any and all contributions, income, accumulations, appreciation, and increase of such retirement benefits after the parties' marriage resulting from ROBERT'S personal services, skill, industry, and efforts, or otherwise, shall be and remain ROBERT'S separate property, and SHIRLEY shall have no right, title, claim, or interest therein. SHIRLEY has been informed by her counsel and understands that pursuant to federal law, or the terms of retirement benefit plan documentation, she may become entitled to survivor rights and/or benefits in, to, or from ROBERT'S retirement benefits. SHIRLEY hereby (a) waives all of her rights to all such survivor benefits under any of ROBERT'S employment benefits; (b) consents to the designation by ROBERT of any person or entity as the beneficiary entitled to any such survivor benefits without further waiver by HER; and (c) agrees to execute all necessary documents within thirty (30) days after marriage in order to effectuate such waiver and consent.

11. Waiver of Rights in Respective Estates: ROBERT and SHIRLEY agree that each party waives and relinquishes, to the fullest extent lawfully possible, all right, title, claim, lien, or interest, whether actual, inchoate, vested, or contingent, in law and equity, under the laws of any state or under federal law, in the other's property, income, and estate by reason of the proposed marriage, including, without limitation, the following:

    a. All community property, quasi-community property, and quasi-marital property rights;

    b. The rights to a probate family allowance;

    c. The rights to a probate homestead;

    d. The rights or claims of dower, curtsy, or any statutory substitute now or hereafter provided under the laws of any state in which the parties may die domiciled or in which they may own real property;

    e. The right to inherit property from the other by intestate succession;

    f. The right to receive property that would pass from the decedent party by testamentary disposition in a will executed before this Agreement;

    g. The right of election to take against the will of the other;

    h. The right to take the statutory share of an omitted spouse;

    i. The right to be appointed as the executor or administrator of the decedent party's estate, except if expressly appointed in a will dated after the date of this Premarital Agreement.

    j. The right to have exempt property set aside;

    k. Any right created under federal law, including, without limitation, the Retirement Equity Act of 1984; and

    l. Any right, title, claim, or interest in or to the property, income, or estate of the other by reason of the parties' nonmarital relationship.

Nothing in this Agreement, however, shall prohibit either party from executing a will after date of this Agreement, and in said will designating the other party as beneficiary, heir, executor, or otherwise. In such event, if said will is dated after the date of this Agreement, the provisions in the will shall supersede paragraph 11 of this agreement.

12. Property Transfers Between Parties: The parties agree that nothing contained in this Agreement shall be construed as a bar to either party's transferring, conveying, devising, or bequeathing any property to the other. Neither party intends by this Agreement to limit or restrict in any way the right to receive any such transfer, conveyance, devise, or bequest from the other made after the parties' marriage. However, the parties specifically agree that no promises of any kind have been made by either of them about any such gift, bequest, devise, conveyance, or transfer from one to the other.

13. Management and Control of Separate Property Interests; Executing Arrangements: The parties agree that each party shall retain and enjoy sole and exclusive management and control of his or her separate property, both during lifetime, and upon death, as though unmarried. In order to accomplish the intent of this Agreement, each of the parties agrees to execute, acknowledge, and deliver, at the request of the other, his or her heirs, executors, administrators, grantees, devisees, or assigns, any and all such deeds, releases, assignments, or other instruments (including, but not limited to, the retirement plan survivor benefits waiver and consent form referred to in paragraph "10" of this Agreement), and such further assurances as may be reasonably required or requested to effect or evidence the release, waiver, relinquishment, or extinguishment of the right of the said party in the property, income, or estate of the other under the provisions of this Agreement and to assure that each party shall have sole and exclusive management and control of his or her separate property.

14. Debt Obligations on Separate Property Interests: All obligations (including principal and interest) incurred due to or as a consequence of the purchase, encumbrance, or hypothecation of the separate property of either party, whether real, personal, or mixed, and all taxes, insurance premiums, and maintenance costs of said separate property, shall be paid from such party's separate property income or from such party's separate property funds, at such party's election, there being no community property by the terms of this Agreement. To the extent that either party uses his or her separate property to pay the foregoing obligations of the other party, there shall be no right to reimbursement for such expenditures.

15. Unsecured Debt Responsibility: All unsecured obligations of each party, no matter when incurred, shall remain the sole and separate obligations of each such party, and each party shall indemnify and hold the other harmless from liability therefor. Each party's unsecured obligations shall be paid from each respective party's separate property income or separate property funds, at such party's election, there

being no community property by the terms of this Agreement. To the extent that either party uses his or her separate property to pay the unsecured obligations of the other party, there shall be no right to reimbursement for such expenditures.

16. Discharge of Living Expenses: The parties' joint living expenses shall be paid from a joint account to be established following the parties' marriage and into which each of the parties shall contribute their salaries from employment during marriage. The term "joint living expenses," as used in this paragraph, includes, but is not limited to: food; household supplies; utilities; telephone; laundry; cleaning; clothing; medical and dental expenses; medical, life, accident, and auto insurance; gasoline, oil, and auto repairs; automobile purchase and/or lease payments; entertainment; support of any minor children that are the issue of the contemplated marriage; and joint gifts to third persons. The commingling of each party's separate property salaries in the aforesaid joint account shall not change the character of such salaries as the contributing party's separate property, and neither party shall acquire any right in the salary of the other by reason of such commingling.

17. Support Liability: Nothing contained in this Agreement shall be construed as absolving either party of the statutory obligation to support the other during marriage or to affect in any way the obligation to support any children of the contemplated marriage. In the event of a separation or marriage dissolution, each party's obligation to support the other shall be determined and governed under the laws of the State of California.

18. Parties and Persons Bound: This Agreement shall bind the parties to the Agreement, and their respective heirs, executors, administrators, assigns, and any other successors in interest.

19. Voluntary Arms' Length Negotiations: The parties acknowledge and agree that this document is voluntarily entered into by and between them and that, as of the date of execution of the Agreement, there is no confidential or fiduciary relationship existing between them as defined under the laws of the State of California. The parties further acknowledge that they have had explained to each of them respectively, by their respective attorneys, the meaning of the terms "confidential relationship" and "fiduciary relationship." The parties specifically acknowledge that neither has ever offered business advice to the other, nor has either become dependent upon the other or relied on the other for advice, and that their relationship as of the date of the execution of this Agreement is a purely personal relationship of two engaged individuals intending to be married to each other at a future date.

20. Execution Formalities: The parties specifically agree that forthwith upon their execution of the Agreement, their respective signatures shall be acknowledged by a notary public in their presence. The parties further acknowledge that the date which is set forth on the first page of this Agreement is the actual date on which they and each of them are signing this Agreement. This Agreement or a memorandum of this Agreement may be recorded at any time and from time to time by either party in any place or office authorized by law for the recording of documents affecting title to or ownership status of property, real or personal, specif-

ically including, but not limited to, any county in which either party resides during the marriage and any county in which either party owns or may own real estate or personal property.

21. Applicable Law: This Agreement is executed in the State of California and shall be subject to and interpreted under the laws of the State of California.

22. Entire Agreement: This Agreement contains the entire understanding and agreement of the parties, and there have been no promises, representations, warranties, or undertakings by either party to the other, oral or written, of any character or nature, except as set forth herein.

23. Modification, Revocation: This Agreement may be altered, amended, modified, or revoked only by an instrument in writing expressly referring to this Agreement, executed, signed, and acknowledged by the parties hereto, and by no other means. Each of the parties waives the right to claim, contend, or assert in the future that this Agreement was modified, cancelled, superseded, or changed by an oral agreement, course of conduct, or estoppel. Both parties agree and state, that on the FIFTH [or TENTH] anniversary of this Agreement, if their marriage is still intact, and no dissolution proceedings have been filed, then, in that event, this Agreement shall be null and void, and from that day on forward, all earnings, skill, service, industry, and effort of each of the parties shall create a community property income, or community property interest, subject to division between the parties.

24. Invalidity, Severability: This agreement has been jointly prepared and negotiated by counsel for each of the parties and shall not be construed against either party. If any term, provision, or condition of this Agreement is held by a court of competent jurisdiction to be invalid, void, or unenforceable, the remainder of the provisions shall remain in full force and effect and shall in no way be affected, impaired, or invalidated.

IN WITNESS WHEREOF, the parties have executed this Premarital Agreement on the date set forth on the first page of this Agreement.

_____
Husband

_____
Wife

_____
Attorney for Husband

_____
Attorney for Wife

(Attach notarization for each party's signature)

HUSBAND'S PROPERTY AND FINANCIAL OBLIGATIONS, Exhibit "A"

WIFE'S PROPERTY AND FINANCIAL OBLIGATIONS,
Exhibit "B"

CARTOON CREDITS

INDEX